PRAISE FOR

Whitney Casey and *The Man Plan*

"Sexy, fun, and outrageous! Whitney taps into all the things men want women to know...Trust me, it's *hot!*"

—Jackie Collins

"She offers up the perfect xo-xo game plan for women."

—*New York Post*

"After reading Whitney Casey's *Man Plan,* you can understand why the former CNN correspondent interviewed more than 250 men in the USA about what turned them on. And off. 'Picky' doesn't begin to capture their demands." —*USA Today*

"*The Man Plan* is the perfect 'companion' for single women— no woman should ever be dateless on a Saturday night again!"

—Match.com

"I wish I'd met Whitney when I was single, or at least had her wisdom in hand. It would have saved me from more than fifty bad blind dates. Whitney is not only gorgeous but effervescent, smart, and savvy. We have worked together from ABC to CNN and everywhere in between, and I have watched her navigate through both politics and pillow talk with grace and ease. She is and always will be the quintessential *Glamour* girl."

—Suze Yalof Schwartz,
executive fashion editor at large of *Glamour* magazine

continued ..

The

MAN
PLAN

Drive Men *Wild*—Not Away

whitney casey

A PERIGEE BOOK

*This book is dedicated
to Houston, Texas,
and all of its "Great Days"*

A PERIGEE BOOK
Published by the Penguin Group
Penguin Group (USA) Inc.
375 Hudson Street, New York, New York 10014, USA
Penguin Group (Canada), 90 Eglinton Avenue East, Suite 700, Toronto, Ontario M4P 2Y3, Canada
(a division of Pearson Penguin Canada Inc.)
Penguin Books Ltd., 80 Strand, London WC2R 0RL, England
Penguin Group Ireland, 25 St. Stephen's Green, Dublin 2, Ireland (a division of Penguin Books Ltd.)
Penguin Group (Australia), 250 Camberwell Road, Camberwell, Victoria 3124, Australia
(a division of Pearson Australia Group Pty. Ltd.)
Penguin Books India Pvt. Ltd., 11 Community Centre, Panchsheel Park, New Delhi—110 017, India
Penguin Group (NZ), 67 Apollo Drive, Rosedale, North Shore 0632, New Zealand
(a division of Pearson New Zealand Ltd.)
Penguin Books (South Africa) (Pty.) Ltd., 24 Sturdee Avenue, Rosebank, Johannesburg 2196,
South Africa

Penguin Books Ltd., Registered Offices: 80 Strand, London WC2R 0RL, England

While the author has made every effort to provide accurate telephone numbers and Internet addresses at the
time of publication, neither the publisher nor the author assumes any responsibility for errors, or for changes
that occur after publication. Further, the publisher does not have any control over and does not assume any
responsibility for author or third-party websites or their content.

PRINTING HISTORY
Perigee hardcover edition / January 2009
Perigee trade paperback edition / January 2010

Perigee trade paperback ISBN: 978-0-399-53577-2

The Library of Congress has cataloged the Perigee hardcover edition as follows:

Casey, Whitney.
    The man plan : drive men wild—not away / Whitney Casey.
        p. cm.
    "A Perigee Book."
    Includes index.
    ISBN 978-0-399-53477-5
    1. Dating (Social customs)—Handbooks, manuals, etc.   2. Man-woman relationships—Handbooks, manu-
als, etc.   I. Title.
    HQ801.C32 2009
    306.73—dc22   2008034417

PRINTED IN THE UNITED STATES OF AMERICA

10 9 8 7 6 5 4 3 2 1

PUBLISHER'S NOTE: The recipe contained in this book is to be followed exactly as written. The publisher is
not responsible for your specific health or allergy needs that may require medical supervision. The publisher is
not responsible for any adverse reactions to the recipe contained in this book.

Most Perigee books are available at special quantity discounts for bulk purchases for sales promotions, pre-
miums, fund-raising, or educational use. Special books, or book excerpts, can also be created to fit specific
needs. For details, write: Special Markets, Penguin Group (USA) Inc., 375 Hudson Street, New York, New
York 10014.

CONTENTS

introduction

Sweetie, women don't want to hear about what other women think. Women want to hear about what *men* think—what men think about their hair, their clothes, their fragrances, their finances, their jobs, the way they are in bed—you name it, women want to know about it...but not from other women." Ugh! She scared me. But she knew what women needed, and she knew how to sell them magazines. As editor in chief of one of the country's top women's magazines, she shocked me with this revelation, explaining that it was information supported by years of research from hundreds of thousands of women who purchased these types of magazines.

Wow! My "rah-rah-go-women-we-can-do-anything" mantra was being muted. Call this crusader crestfallen. For weeks I had been submitting story ideas and articles for her magazine. Nothing was making it to print. Mine were insightful stories of women helping other women to be their best and triumph over men or adversity. I thought my stories were inspiring and riveting; Ms. Editor in Chief did not.

Could it really be true? Had my hardworking, indepen-dent, and educated single sisterhood truly traded in their books and briefcases for Barbies? If her magazine was right, then—doll or no doll—"Ken" mattered. It was then that I realized that if I wanted to make it into her magazine, or into a man's heart, Ken and his cohorts would have to be heard. This was the genesis of *The Man Plan*.

Who Cares What He Thinks, Anyway?

Just as it had irked me, the idea of really caring about what men think (and then doing something to change yourself based on that information) may cut you to the core. Despite Ms. Edi-tor in Chief's fancy research, why should you care about what a man thinks about you? And, more important, why should you change yourself based on what men think? You are "you," and nobody should influence that, right? Wrong. Apparently, if you want a man, you need a plan.

Think about this question in a different context. If you really wanted a certain job, would you go on an interview for that job without studying the company's founding philosophies and researching its CEO? Of course not! You would devise a plan of attack. You would read up, study up, ask around, and infuse yourself into that company's world so as to appear as if you seamlessly fit into its fold. You would find people who had worked for or knew a lot about that company. You would know what to wear on the interview, what to say, and how to convince them you are the perfect candidate for that job.

The same process and plan should be used with a man. You need to do your research and know what to wear, what to say, what to smell like, and how to convince him that you are the perfect candidate for...him. You can decide if he's a fit for you later, but gaining access to his "company" is the first step.

Every CEO or HR person will tell you that the initial interview is the wooing process, not the wowing process. It is the time you need to fit in and mesh with the company. Men need to be wooed before they are wowed; they need to see how you will fit in and mesh with them. When you actually get the job you want (or the man you want) and begin to establish yourself, then you can use your individualism, creativity, and personality to move forward and make an impact on the company (or on his heart). But first things first—you need to get the job (and the man!).

With this book in hand, you have the stealthy and all-important insider's information it takes to get that man. You will know how to drive men wild and make them want you. You will be hired, not fired.

Toe the Line

There is a fine line between wooing, wowing, and then possibly shooing them away. That line has to be defined and followed. Whether you are seeking a job, a date, or a mate, or are married or wanting to be married, defining what entices, attracts, and draws men in is one of the most essential elements to getting exactly what you want from men.

You will learn these essentials in the following chapters of *The Man Plan*. The purpose of this book is twofold: it will give you the tools to master what it takes to drive men wild, while also educating you on what drives them away. These tenets are not just my opinions on the aforementioned. My dating life could be either very similar to yours or very different. It depends on what we have already experienced, learned, and then applied in our individual love lives. Instead of guesswork and single-sided opining, I went straight to the source... men. I tackled the research for this book much like I took on the research for the stories I covered as a hard-hitting journalist for CNN. No report should be based on secondhand information when the real deal is available.

I canvassed the current male opinions and atmosphere, interviewing men from every socioeconomic background and age group, from urban to urbane and from St. Louis to SoHo. I then whittled away at the information, getting to the top recurring factors that drove men away. Finally, I honed in on the factors that compelled men to stay. It was real shoe-leather reporting—just the facts, ma'am—fair and balanced. (Fair like a fox and balanced on four-inch stilettos!)

From a woman's breath to her breasts, the chapters all start with a story of what went wrong in a man's mind. Although the stories may exasperate you, they are meant to liberate you instead. They are true male tales from the trenches, relayed at times with shocking irreverence and brutal honesty. If you choose not to take any of the book's advice, you will (at least) be entertained by the anecdotal field evidence straight from the horse's mouth. For every man's flaw-filled story of what went south with a woman, there are spades of solutions on how to make it go exactly the way a woman wants. He may be navigating, but you're driving.

The stories in this book come from real men. In addition, the solutions come from some of the world's leading experts in all fields of study or practice. I interviewed more than 250 men across the country and sought out advice for what they considered "fatal female flaws" by interviewing dozens of doctors, psychologists, fashionistas, and financiers. Every aspect of what lures a man in and makes him crazy about a woman is covered and... um...uncovered. From pro athletes and pastors to supermodels and strippers, *The Man Plan* explores all avenues of advice, input, and information. With the likes of P. Diddy, Emeril Lagasse, supermodel Karolina Kurková, pastor Joel Osteen, and Dr. Laura Berman, it is truly a collection of unconventional wisdom combined with unbelievably honest and brutal details.

All Senses and No Sensibility

In the pages ahead you will discover that getting the guy or driving the one you already have wild is all about appealing to his senses, *not* his sensibilities. A man's senses always trump his sensibilities. Your plan starts here. The conversation and communication aspect of a man is moot. If you can't "pass go and collect $200" in the first part of his game—his senses—then you shouldn't even attempt to play the rest of the game. You have to get the first move right. This is imperative to master on initial contact with a man.

A lot of books will focus your attention on how a man is emotionally wired. These theories are the quickest way to a short circuit and a major "male-function." The take-home on men is simple. *The Man Plan* will teach you that the most important thing you should know about a man is this: When it comes to women—if men like what they see, smell, touch, and taste, they'll take it. Get this part nailed down and you will conquer, win, and land any man.

You will have the confidence of knowing that you have done everything right to make him "Mr. Right Now." It will then be up to you (not him) to decide whether you want to move him from "Mr. Right Now" to "Mr. Right."

So enjoy the journey. With every turn of the page it is sure to be an adventurous one. *The Man Plan* will give you all you need to drive men wild, not away. If you follow the plan, you will drive away knowing you have him—and, being in the driver's seat, it will be you who will choose whether he'll be riding shotgun.

Note: The stories in the book are true stories. However, the names have been changed at the request of the interviewees.

STEP ONE

PICK AN OUTFIT

Getting His Once-Over
on Fashion and Style

one

Clothing and Accessories

Undressing Your Dressing

It was a blind date for Mike. He picked the restaurant—a laid-back and cozy place that he had been to a handful of times. He wasn't nervous.

On the other hand, his date, Jennifer, had just spent the last thirty minutes undergoing thirty wardrobe changes; all seemed to be malfunctioning. She was running out of time and hated being late for their first date. She decided on outfit change number fifteen. It seemed halfway between the way she really wanted to dress and the way she thought she ought to dress for a first date.

Change number fifteen did not land her a perfect ten, however. As she walked through the restaurant's bar looking for Mike, her black, super-stomach-sucking-in, knee-length pencil skirt began to hike up her knees to her thighs as if it were a Ferrari racing from her hemline to her waistline. Just as she thought it was okay to shimmy it back down her legs, Mike stood up to introduce himself. Too late! Now they had to walk to their table. She tried to walk slowly as Mike followed her, and she knew he was looking at her behind, which was about to show everything under its hood. She made it to the finish line. But so did her hemline. By the time she needed to sit, her skirt was ready to split, which is exactly what happened.

Warning: Slippery When Worn

In hopes of avoiding fashion accidents like Jennifer's, a well-thought-out set of style directions is needed. From head to toe and all the accessories in between, you need to be completely comfortable and self-assured with your wardrobe choices. Men feel this comfort level. They know when you aren't feelin' it. Warning: "Comfort" isn't the same thing as saying "you need to wear something comfortable." Often the perfect outfit to woo a man may not be the most comfortable. But you have to be comfortable with its uncomfortableness.

The comfort you'll own is more about knowing ahead of time how things move and work on you. You have to know your clothes and accessories—what they are going to do, what they are going to say (they can be pretty loud sometimes, literally), and how they are going to move. The ultimate goal is to harness your self-confidence even if it means harnessing in your wardrobe choices.

A man will never say, "She was acting weird because she didn't feel comfortable in the skirt she had on," or, "Her accessories were making a lot of noise, and I think they made her aware that I didn't like them." They aren't aware of what wardrobe malfunctions are afflicting you while you are with them. Instead, they may note, "She was acting weird; I don't know why. Maybe she isn't the one for me." A bad impression can make a man move on quickly, so it is time to get comfortable with your getup.

Directions from a Fashion Traffic Stop

Singles expert, style guru, and author Jerusha Stewart has made it her life's mission to get women into their true and sexy comfort zone. When it comes to fashion, her tips for finding the perfect fit will fix any fashion foibles and focus his attention on you, not the skirt that is riding up your leg the wrong way. According to Jerusha, it just takes seven steps to self-confident and sexy man-dressing!

1. **Don't wear black.** Your mission is to stand out, not blend in with your surroundings. (An unofficial poll of single guys found that they find black totally desperate—and boring.)

2. **Don't wear your closet.** This is not the time to layer your favorite shirt underneath that gorgeous sweater you just couldn't resist at the mall and cover them with ropes of chains and pearls. With that much eye candy, your guy may have trouble figuring out where to focus.

3. **Don't show up in anything that makes you look like you've been wrapped, twisted, or tied up in knots.** This only leads to wrong-way thinking on his part, such as, "How did she get into that getup...and how am I supposed to get her out of it?"

4. **Focus on looking great above the waist.** Chances are, most of the evening you'll be sitting down. Give him something to talk about: a blouse in a great color, a well-made top that shows off your shoulders, or jeweled earrings that catch the light.

5. **Embrace color.** You don't have to dress in a Technicolor splash, but a little color around your face will bring out your eyes and your smile. Adopt a signature shade. Use the rich hue to get up close and personal.

6. **Fit and flatter.** Don't worry about size; focus on fit. When the dress is on you, it should fit you and not your imaginary size.

7. **Last, a first date is not the same as the big reveal.** Flaunt your best features but not all of them at once. A plunging neckline does not need to compete with a thigh-high skirt. Less is more. The less you show now, the more you'll have for later.

Caught on Camera

Jerusha also suggests spending some time in your closet with a friend who will be lovingly honest with you about how you look in different ensembles. Pick three different outfits from casual to dressy that make you feel like a rock star (and that your friend agrees make you look like a rock star, too). Also pick the shoes and accessories to go with the outfits.

Take Polaroids or digital pictures of the outfits and keep them for when you need to get ready for that first date. You will not only save time but also save yourself all the anxiety by knowing that these outfits look good, fit correctly, and won't ride up your thighs.

Accessorizing for the Finish Line

Now that you have your outfits in place, it's time to take a look at what you're adding to the mix that may be mixing him up. The challenge is to find out which "shiny thing" can distract or, better yet, attract him.

Enlisted for this challenge is Sylvana Soto-Ward, *Vogue* magazine's 2007 accessories editor. Sylvana explains that a woman's accessories have to serve a purpose. Sylvana adds that men can understand and notice a woman's accessories if she does it right. And doing it right starts with a little geometry. Sylvana says the better way to think about accessorizing for a man is to do it in "planes," or regions of the body. Each accessory fits on or in a specific plane of the body. For instance, if you have earrings on, skip the necklace and wear a cuff; therefore, you are only putting emphasis on one plane at a time. Men aren't good multitaskers. Each accessory is considered a task for them. They look at it and think, "What is that shiny thing on her? Why is it clacking, jingling, or sparkling?" If you give them too many tasks in one region, it just ends up confusing and distracting them. No more than three planes (or parts of the body) is a good rule to adhere to when it comes to jewelry and men.

Making Noise for the Boys

Anything that creates a cacophony, whether it is your bangles or your belt, has got to stay home. It can make all the noise it wants in your jewelry box, but while out with a man, loud noises are just turnoffs. Again, it is another task they have to sift through on you. Switch out the bangles for a large cuff or nothing at all.

Another big no-no for men is wearing matching sets of jewelry. Sylvana explains: "It is old-fashioned to wear jewelry in sets. It is too matchy. You can still buy sets and keep the ones you have, but mix them up when you wear them out. Even try mixing gold and silver pieces together." Men perceive matching accessories as matronly, which can add a few years to your age because, heck, as boys, their moms were way older than them...right?

Speaking of old, when it comes to Grandma Gerty's vintage brooch or pin, Sylvana says, "Keep those as keepsakes. Men don't understand those types of sentimental pieces. They only see 'old and dated'—not sexy and fresh." Also, when it comes to statement pieces—for example, pieces that say "I'm bohemian" or "I'm for peace"—Sylvana says to leave them at home. It doesn't mean you are abandoning your style altogether; it just means you aren't telling all up front. A woman's mystery can be one of her best accessories when it comes to attracting a man.

Another hard and fast rule when it comes to bling and boys: "No pearls. They are boring, too conservative, and should only be worn to church or to meet the parents." Again, men pull from the cadre of memories they hold of the women who participated in their lives while growing up. Their Sunday school teacher wore pearls, or maybe it was their aunt Betty, who knitted those horrible sweaters they had to wear every holiday. You get the picture. He sees it on you and his subconscious recollects very unsexy sensations! However, Sylvana concedes that if you have a real penchant for pearls, then wear a great pair of dangly pearl earrings or chandelier earrings with pearls. This will help update your accessories look even if you can't put the pearl out to pasture. Dangly earrings draw a man's eyes toward your décolletage, a super-sexy spot for his subconscious.

From Chic to Chintzy

Ah...the décolletage, a hot spot for men that women need to focus on. The space between your shoulders horizontally and from your neck to your breasts laterally is one of the most sensual parts of the body for him and is generally a place that is beautiful and perfect on every woman.

Be warned: Don't overdo the décolletage. Sylvana says this is a sure way to cheapen your look. If right below the décolletage you have great cleavage, she says you should never wear something dangling down in it. "That's the fastest way to go from elegance to chintzy. It is not chic to be so blatant about your best asset," says Sylvana. Instead she suggests that if you have a great cleavage, you should try to emphasize the décolletage and collarbone area. This can be accomplished by wearing a long or dangly earring to draw the eyes down, but not too far to where it gets tacky and too suggestive. In other words, if there is something you like on your body (such as your cleavage), don't flaunt it—flaunt something next to it.

A Watch for Function and Fashion

Finally, there is one accessory all men truly understand. If you are to invest in any type of pricy long-term accessory, it should be a good watch. A watch can be timeless and can give you instant credibility. Men know watches; they respect them. However, Sylvana advises, "Don't wear a watch when attending a formal or if you are on a sexy or romantic date with a man." Wearing a watch to a cocktail party or black-tie event or into the wee hours of the night can look like you aren't ready for adventure or excitement. You shouldn't be looking at your watch at one of these events anyway...where do you need to go? You are so fabulous, time doesn't matter!

Clothing the Deal

When it comes to accessorizing and dressing to attract that man, take your clothing and accessories on a test run, so that when you do wear them, you're so comfortable, you feel as if you were born to seduce and conquer him. Go ahead, bling up your best asset. Jump in that jewelry box and closet and go get him.

two

Handbags and Shoes

Be a "Shoe-in"
Who's Got It "In the Bag"

Melissa was running late and didn't have a chance to go home and change before her date. She was already wearing a cute and sexy dress under her more conservative work blazer, so she felt as if her outfit was good enough. She had on a sexy pair of new stilettos and was accessorized, perfumed, and carrying her new oversize Marc Jacobs handbag. She was just grabbing drinks, and it was only a second date—no need to overthink things.

She arrived on time, meeting Damien at the bar. Whew! She was relieved. He had come from work, too. She ordered a cocktail. But while she was waiting for her drink to arrive, Damien seemed uncomfortable. He was a bit fidgety and seemed to want to ask her something. When they got their drinks and were getting ready to walk over to one of the bar tables to sit down, Damien made a comment that revealed the cause of his distraction.

"Melissa, why don't you take the drinks, and I will carry your luggage to the table."

"Luggage? I'm not going anywhere."

"Oh, I am so sorry; I thought you might be going on a business trip or coming back from one when I saw your bag."

Melissa was mortified, but Damien was curious. What was in that giant bag? Why did she need it with her on their date? Was she sleeping over at someone else's house? Was she hiding a small child? Was she assuming she'd be sleeping at his place?

The Answer: It's in the Bag

If only Melissa had talked with one of the country's leading handbag experts, Anna Johnson, or at least read her book *Handbags: The Power of the Purse*. Johnson says that after researching handbags and men by the droves, she's discovered that women like Melissa are sending a loud message to their dates. "When women like Melissa either knowingly or unwittingly bring out a large and heavy bag on a date, they are saying to men, 'I can look after myself. I don't need you. I have my survival pack right here on my shoulder.'" The big bag implies "I can do everything." But, Anna admonishes, "that means she will spend the rest of her life doing everything...herself."

Instead, she suggests that when women pick a handbag for a date, the bag should be smaller, dainty, and more precise. Anna says during courtship women should exaggerate their femininity, and she believes a woman's handbag can be a great place to start. "Your handbag can be an opportunity to show off your personality," she says. "I'm not suggesting you should bust out your kitschy Hello Kitty bag, but maybe add color, bedazzle, or sport the animal print with your bag. It can be a great conversation starter, as it isn't too distracting because it is small, but it just adds a little zip to your zaza!"

In hopes of avoiding Melissa's mishap, Anna suggests an arm test. If you reach into your bag and your bag covers the area of your wrist to your elbow, then "that's not a handbag. That's luggage! It doesn't belong on a date." She also says that even if your bag is too big and you decide to carry it on a date, you should carry it yourself: "A man should never carry a woman's handbag for her. That is tantamount to carrying her shirt, cigarette, perfume, or diary. A woman's handbag is one of her most personal assets."

Your Dating Handbag of Tricks

If a woman's bag truly is one of her most personal and powerful assets, then the bag's contents should have a few secret male-catching weapons at the ready. Besides the typical touch-up makeup, wallet, perfume, and phone, what else should be in the bag? Anna suggests putting in some props—things you can use if the conversation gets stale or you need to facilitate the date—like an article you've pulled out of the *Economist*, an interesting stat from a book you've just read, a grade-school picture your mother just sent you, a Magic 8-Ball key chain that can help predict the future, or a book from the series of small books called *101 Questions You Want Answered*. Sometimes it takes men a little while to feel comfortable talking about personal things, so if you are feeling this, just whip out your purse prop and get down to business with interesting conversation that just popped out of your purse.

Finally, one of the best items to keep in your bag-o-tricks is something that reminds you of who you are and why you are great. Anna believes women can often worry so much about the style of their bag, their style, their date, and what he thinks about them that they forget who they are and why they are so great. For this reason, she suggests throwing something in your handbag that makes you remember exactly who you are, how great you are, and how every man should fall head over heels for you. Maybe you have a fabulous fortune from a fortune cookie that actually came true, a picture of you winning a Pulitzer, a perfume sample that reminds you of a time in your life when all was perfect, a rabbit's foot, or a pair of dice. Whatever it is, all it has to do is give you a little boost of confidence. Men love self-confident women.

Best Foot Backward

Before you run away together with your fabulous bag and your self-confidence, you may want to take a look south. Your feet may be barking back at you, saying some things you would rather he not hear. It's time to get the right fit now, so that you will be sure to be a "shoe-in" with men anytime.

Betsy picked her favorite navy blue vintage Ferragamo flats, replete with the trademark, perfectly placed navy blue grosgrain bow, fastened with the timeless small gold plate in the middle. She felt comfy in these shoes and knew that her date, David, was a little shorter than her; the combo would make for a good fit in footwear. So she thought. David didn't dig it. "Her shoes screamed silence! Like a mean and unsexy librarian." David also explained that her shoes seemed unadventurous and reminded him of his grade-school Catholic nuns. There was no way Betsy could be the "footloose and fancy-free" fun woman he wanted to date in those shoes. He never once thought she might be wearing flats because he was shorter than her and she was considerate of him. Instead, he imagined her potential flaws.

With the exception of extreme shoe-fetish types, most men are somewhat like David when it comes to shoes. They couldn't really tell you the brand or style of the shoe a woman is wearing, but they can tell you if it makes a woman look more sexy and attracts their attention. Men want you to put your best foot forward, but only if that foot is ready to rock a sexy sensation.

She's the Real Heel

Author Meghan Cleary is one of the country's only "shoe therapists." She's made a successful career out of coaching women on how to pick the perfect pair and wear them with the perfect panache. Meghan jokes that when it comes to men and shoes, "Flats may level the playing field. But who wants to do that?" Meghan says that for men, a flat, especially the iconic Ferragamo flats previously mentioned, harks back to a conservative old-world thought process. A walk in those types of shoes may make him think you are too conservative and not spontaneous enough. Instead, Meghan suggests, "When you want to feel great, you've got to elevate."

According to Meghan, the reasons for "moving up" in the world have more to do with the message your body language sends in heels than the message your physical body sends. Yes, heels elongate a woman's legs, move the pelvis slightly forward, and create a sleeker look, but Meghan says that's just the beginning. It's what's going on inside the woman's psyche when she elevates that makes the heel the real deal. Meghan explains, "When women put on heels their body responds, making a physical shift, but her mind follows in tow. Wearing heels causes women to send out myriad signals of confidence, femininity, and strength. Women, metaphorically, stand taller by projecting themselves as more composed and assertive."

Men respond not only to the physical aspect of the stilettos but, even more, to the confidence projected by the woman wearing them. The heel is aesthetically pleasing to men, but the woman who is confident in her newly heightened femininity is even more alluring.

Go Ahead! Let the Other Shoe Drop

What if walking in heels is your Achilles' heel? No worries. Meghan suggests wearing a streamlined wedge or a shorter heel with a platform; either will still elevate you both mentally and physically. She advises steering clear of any type of shoe that is bulky, clunky, complicated, or cumbersome, such as an espadrille or a heavy boot. She also warns, "Unless you are absolutely proficient and adept at walking in them, and you are sure your date isn't below average in the height category, wearing skyscraper type stilettos is a no-no." And she adds another cautionary foot faux pas: "Unless you are Cinderella, clear shoes probably won't woo your Prince Charming." What seems sexy in the strip clubs, in *Playboy* magazine, and on pinups should be left there.

So, if a woman is to have only one pair of shoes to wear when she goes out with a man, what would it be? Meghan advises that women should pick a basic black mid-heel silhouette with a cone heel of about two and a half inches. So as not to date the shoe, she also advises choosing an almond-shaped toe or, for spring and summer, a peep-toe sandal with the same two-and-a-half-inch cone heel.

You're a "Shoe-in"

Meghan also points out that Prince Charming may or may not notice you've just spent some major Benjamins on your latest and greatest Louboutins, but he will notice how confident your new heightened state has made you. So keep it on the up and up, rock that stiletto, and no matter how bad your date or man ends up acting, at least you'll know you're well heeled and the one who's got a leg up. The combo of your sexy-looking legs, the perfect pump, and that handy handbag will make any man say, "Bag it up . . . I'll take it."

three

Nipples, Lingerie, and Hosiery

Out-of-Control-Top Pantyhose and What to Wear Under There

Charlie is a quintessential metrosexual. His hair is always perfectly coiffed; his nails are clean, shiny, and always buffed; and his *très* chic clothing is exactly tailored to his svelte and sinewy frame. Enter Rachel. Her hair is always a little off, she's lucky when her nails are all the same length, and she irons her clothes because they are generally at the bottom of her laundry basket for a week. The two could not be more different but had begun to try out a fledgling courtship.

Charlie's persnickety perfection gave Rachel a huge complex. Every time she dressed for their dates, she changed ten times from top to bottom. One night she decided to don a summery orange strapless number with a high waistline. She thought a pair of cute cotton boy shorts under the dress would make her feel more secure than a normal thong.

After she arrived, it was not more than five minutes before Charlie's hand accidentally brushed her thigh. He felt the boy shorts and asked Rachel, "What the heck are you wearing under there?" She explained to him what boy shorts are, to which he responded, "So basically you are wearing tighty whities for women! Who in their right mind would invent those for women to wear? They aren't even remotely sexy." Rachel was upset; Charlie was turned off. It wasn't pretty, and there would be no sex (or sexy) in that city.

The "Box" Populi

That was one man, one city, but what is the vox populi on what to wear under there? A quick polling of men from all over the country finds the following commentary on the question, Do men really notice lingerie, and if so, what kind?

BRIAN, Detroit: "I love to see women in lingerie. It has a different effect according to what they are wearing, and what they have on their minds while wearing it."

CHRIS, Omaha: "Nice lingerie is sexy and a great way for her to express her feelings, or to just be a little daring...which is adventurous and attractive."

SHANE, Florida: "I like to see my girl in lingerie for two reasons. First, it lets me know that she's interested so I don't have to guess. Second, lingerie adds mystery. Even though I've seen everything before, it looks different in lingerie."

JEREMIAH, San Diego: "Yes, of course! That is the most common fantasy of a man. To undress a woman, especially her lingerie, you have the dream of doing it very softly to see her nude."

CLYDE, Seattle: "I love it. It really does matter. If I'm with a girl, no matter how attractive she is, if she takes off her pants and she's wearing those big Hanes panties, it really works to dampen the mood."

JD, Massachusetts: "Lingerie is like a beautiful frame on a fantastic work of art. Of course, being a guy, it's also reminiscent of Christmas wrapping on a great present."

SALAAM, Austin: "Teddies in metallic colors, like blue and green, always get me fired up."

Lingerie for Foreplay, Not Function

So, from men in Massachusetts to San Diego, there is no question a little lingerie goes a long way. Men want to believe that all women wake up and put on a matching set of sexy lingerie for that just-in-case encounter with them. They think of your undergarments in terms of foreplay, not function. If there is a chance they get to catch a glance, or they happen to brush by your leg and feel something sexy, their imagination runs wild. The thought of you needing a basic nude bra without seams to go under that blouse (although practical to you) is not sexy to them at all. They want to think you have on a frilly lacy number.

Lingerie serves another function. Even if no one sees or feels it but you, sexy lingerie works wonders for your body language and self-confidence. He may never know that you are rockin' that little red lacy set underneath your clothes, but you do. You can choose to let him in on the sexy secret later, or you can choose to stay coy and keep your secret to yourself. You will walk and act a little more self-confidently and seductively, and he won't even know why.

Titillating Tricks of the Trade

Two women who know a lot about the power of the panty and the best way to attract a man with what you wear under there are Susan Nethero and Monica Mitro. As the author of *Bra Talk*, Susan has been dubbed "the bra whisperer." She has fit more than 100,000 women in bras across the country. Monica also has a slew of secrets to sexy. She works with some of the biggest supermodels at one of the largest and most well-known lingerie brands in the world—Victoria's Secret. Monica offers her insight: "Men aren't educated enough on the technical aspects of panties and bras such as underwire, push-up wireless, et cetera. For men, it's about what they see on the outside." Susan agrees: "A little hint of lingerie dancing out of your low-cut blouse can pique a man's interest and add a little drama to your dinner."

However, lingerie can also malfunction when it comes to men. Susan and Monica say there are seven things women do wrong when picking just what to wear under there.

Say No to Nude

Nude lingerie to a man translates as boring and bland. If you have to go with a nude, Susan suggests finding a nude "date" bra: a bra that has some lace on the edges or an interesting nude pattern on pattern, or the bra could even be a sheer nude with a beautiful gold, crystal, or floral clasp in the middle.

Don't Sport the Sports Bra

Both Susan and Monica agree: "Keep the sports bra in the gym." If you need a seamless look for a T-shirt, or a sweater, Susan suggests trying out the seamless bras that are usually designed for T-shirt-wearing women.

Too Much Padding and Adding

You can fake the eye, but when you fake the guy too much, he gets a little upset. If you are putting drastic size enhancers, contraptions, or other products into your bra before your date, then you are really faking the guy out. Susan says you don't need all of those add-ons anyway: "Eighty-five percent of women wear the wrong bra size. If they found the right one, it would work wonders for their self-confidence and their breasts."

The Oh-No-You-Di'n't Granny Panty

Every woman knows the comfort of a great pair of cotton undies—the pair you wear when you just don't have time to do your laundry. *No way,* says Monica. "Granny panties are definitely not sexy! If a woman likes a fuller panty style, I'd recommend a hip hugger. It gives fuller coverage, plus usually has cute style—and you can find a fun print." Men can understand a fun print, but if it looks like it may have belonged to them (the tighty-whitey boy shorts), it's a total buzz bust.

Mismatching Tops and Bottoms

"Matching is key," says Susan. "Men don't really understand or care that it is sometimes hard for women to find the perfect panty-bra match and make it fit perfectly, too, but they want you to have it." Pick the set if possible. Monica agrees that men do prefer it when their lady's lingerie matches, but when in a pinch, "picking a novelty-type pair of panties with cute, flirty details that don't necessarily have bras to match is one backup—as long as the bra you pick has some of the colors in it that the panty has."

Nippleless Women and Nipple Slips

Another one of the top mistakes women make when it comes to their putting their best assets forward is a phenomenon known as the nippleless woman. Susan says, "Women should realize that the natural form of their breast is a sexy thing. The nipple is natural. We weren't born without them! So flaunt them." However, Susan also warns, "Save the headlights for the night. There is plenty of light at your office or at the company picnic. Do the dimmer in the day." Whatever you decide, keep the following tips in mind:

• Never go braless. Nipples are hot; saggy breasts are not.

• As a general rule, nips should not come out before 9:00 p.m., unless it's one of the special occasions noted below.

• Places to nip: casinos, nightclubs, wine bars, bars, concerts, the beach (after 3:00 p.m.), driving in a convertible, outdoor sporting events (baseball games are an exception, as there are generally a lot of children), evening wedding receptions (only if there are a cache of available men), a girls' weekend in Vegas.

• Places not to nip: wedding ceremonies and dinners, grocery stores, lunch dates, hair salons, dinner dates before 9:00 p.m., work, the gym, the PTA, a small neighborhood or apartment pool, the opera, the ballet, Broadway shows, charity events, galas and awards ceremonies, anywhere small children could stare.

Nude Hosiery and the Out-of-Control-Top Pantyhose

One of the final foibles on the list of what not to wear under there comes in the form of form-fitting pantyhose, tights, and all other types of hosiery. Arden Hess-Rowland is a hosiery expert for Wolford, one of the world's leading lines of ladies hosiery. She suggests women approach buying leg wear like they do cosmetics. "Think of it as makeup for our legs." Men don't love a lot of makeup, and the same holds true for the legs. Arden says nothing ages a woman faster than wearing dark skin–toned pantyhose. "Would you match your pale skin with a dark foundation? Men don't think it is flattering when they see a pale woman wearing dark tan hosiery." Talk about mismatched!

Another part of pantyhose, tights, or hosiery in general that is incredibly unsexy is the formidable control top. The control top triggers images of girdles and grannies. Plus, if your stomach or sides overflow, the unsexy factor increases exponentially for men. Most men admit they understand that women want to look thinner, but what they don't understand is the contraptions involved in that quest—the control top being one of them. Squishing yourself into the control top is something you can do for the boardroom, but it won't get him to the bedroom. The way to go is thigh highs.

That may seem intimidating, but Arden says not all thigh highs come with moving parts. Garters, snaps, bows, and belts can be sexy but not always practical. Some men actually fear all those bells and whistles. "Stay ups" are the way to go. They are thigh highs with a little rubbery material around the top that grabs on to the thigh and sends your sexiness to the sky! Arden warns, "Make sure you buy the correct size; if they fit you, they won't cause an indentation on your skin and you won't spill out over them—never pretty."

She's Got Legs and Knows How to Use Them

When it comes to a final list of things to love about your legs and what to put on in hopes of putting on his passion for you, Arden has a final checklist every woman should walk through. These steps will lead you to a leg that is a lean, mean man-catching machine:

- For winter, when picking tights, go with matte, opaque, semi-sheer; anything black.

- If you have to wear nude, try a tone-on-tone pattern, small woven lines, or a lacy type.

- Avoid too much color. Men don't want to date a Smurf or Strawberry Shortcake.

- Avoid anything too shiny—especially for the day.

- No loud prints or stripes that run straight across the leg or straight up and down. The Cat in the Hat is still single...wonder why?

- Open-toe shoes should be worn with sandal-toe tights, or go without. No exceptions. Take note of your toes, too...every man will look at those funky feet, so get them cleaned up before even attempting this one.

- Peep-toe shoes (if in style) can be worn with opaque tights. If in doubt, wear black.

Leggo His Ego

Okay, now you're ready to walk it, work it, and own it (and him). You've got your perfect panty and bodacious bra; you know the tips of when to nip and when not to nip; and nothing beats your great pair of legs. You now know what to wear under there—he doesn't stand a chance.

SHOWER

The Down and Dirty
on Health and Hygiene

four

Body Odor
and Bad Breath

Sweating the Small Stuff on Smell

Betsy was a tall blonde with a rockin' body. She worked out at her gym with a personal trainer three times a week. Tony was her trainer. Then it was Nick. Then Kevin, Joe, Jason, Dom, and Phil followed. Despite her undeniable hotness, the entire personal training staff at her gym in New Jersey couldn't commit to training Betsy. Why? "She stunk!"

According to the bevy of buff boys at her beck and call, beautiful Betsy had a bit of a sweating problem. "When she would call for an appointment, we would all rock-paper-scissors each other to see who had to train her that day." Apparently, withstanding the whiffs of rank wafting from Betsy's body was too much heavy lifting, even for a skilled weight lifter. Betsy quickly became dubbed "Sweatsy." Sweatsy never knew why she had a rotating roster of trainers (and boyfriends), but it is rumored Sweatsy got the hint and now smells of mint.

Sniffing You Out

One of the most powerful attractors for a man is his nose. He may not be able to smell that *he* smells, but for some reason he always knows when a woman does. A man doesn't mind seeing his woman glisten à la Olivia Newton John in her 1980s "Physical" video, but when it comes to good old-fashioned sweat drops and smell, he'd rather take a pass than make a pass at you. For a man, a woman's armpits, hands, and feet should all exist as odor-free, sweat-free regions.

So what's a stinky girl to do? You can't stop sweating because, seriously, the sweatless woman doesn't exist and is clearly not a healthy option—or a practical one, for that matter. But there are some key ways in which women can stop the sweat and the stifling smell that comes along with it.

Dermatologist Sherry Novick has treated many a sweaty patient without even breaking a sweat. But if she were to sweat, she says knowing a woman's body and the way it sweats is the real way to keeping on your man plan. If you know how it works, then you'll know how to stop it and keep him from running the other way. First thing to know is that there are two main culprits working in your body when it comes to losing your cool: the eccrine and apocrine glands (your sweat glands). Those suckers stick together when it comes to not smelling so swell. But one has a little more kick.

Your eccrine sweat glands function to maintain your body temperature and are located over your entire body surface. They are most concentrated on the palms of your hands and the soles of your feet. These lovely little gems are your "nervous narcs"; they let every man know when you aren't sure of him or yourself. They make you sweat if you are under emotional or mental stress and anxiety, or if you are hot or overheated. "What most people don't know is that when they start sweating, these eccrine sweat glands secrete sweat that is clear, watery, odorless, and sterile," explains Dr. Novick. "The actual sweat excreted onto the skin is odorless. In general, when you speak of being wet and 'sweaty,' you are referring to eccrine sweat production."

The Pit-iful Truth

Your apocrine sweat glands are the second smoking gun in the stink game. These glands are located in your armpits, and also surround your genitals and your nipples. These aren't things he knows, but his nose does! Apocrine sweat glands continuously produce small amounts of an oily fluid. As with the eccrine sweat, the sweat produced by apocrine glands is also colorless, odorless, and sterile. However, normal bacterial decomposition of this type of sweat on your skin produces what we typically smell (body odor). Poor personal hygiene then causes more and a stronger odor. He'll turn his nose up if you don't listen up to how to fix this for sure.

According to Dr. Novick, people who suffer from oversweating of the armpits do not smell more than the people who sweat normally. This oversweating phenomena is actually a condition called axillary hyperhidrosis, and it generally occurs as a reaction to your emotions and anxiety levels. He can sniff this anxiety out without a doubt. The more anxious or emotional you become, the more you sweat. The more you sweat, the more he'll know you're sweating via your clammy hands, funky feet, and unpretty pit stains. But hey...don't sweat it, because you may be sweaty, but at least he can't smell you. You aren't stinky. "In fact, the excess sweat you make with your eccrine sweat glands [mentioned above] tends to wash away the stink-producing apocrine sweat we all produce."

PMSweat Time of the Month

Speaking of getting emotional, how about that lovely time of the month when women have their periods. Ugh! Do men know we are hanging with Aunt Flo? "Women do have some variation in sweating during their menstrual cycles." Dr. Novick says that when a woman is in the preovulatory phase of the menstrual cycle, she will sweat more in response to heat and exertion (like exercise) because of increased basal body temperature during this phase of the cycle. This is why women should take a little break, regroup, and then get their A game back on after that time of the month.

When it comes to other factors upping your sweat, Dr. Novick adds smoking to the list of culprits: "Stimulating substances such as nicotine and caffeine can make you sweat more. Other sweaty stuff includes stress and certain medications." So now that you are sweating over all of this, just add some garlic to the recipe and, voilà, you've got a stewing stench secreted straight from your sweat. Bon appétit! You won't be his sweet treat for the night!

So how do you avoid the smell and stay like a flower all day in his presence? Since Bacteria + Moisture (Sweat) = Body Odor, you want to stay as dry as possible. Store-bought, over-the-counter antiperspirants are typically composed of aluminum salts, which inhibit the production of sweat when applied (keeping you dry), thereby also inhibiting the production of body odor by eliminating the moist surface needed for bacteria to create an unfortunate scent.

Natural deodorants often contain alum, which is a derivative of the aluminum salts in most other deodorants. However, the ingredients in natural deodorants are not absorbed into the skin like typical aluminum. Instead, they exert their effect by slowing or stopping some bacterial growth on the skin. Therefore, natural deodorants are typically not as effective. You may be one of those au naturel women, but there is nothing natural about a man staying around to stop and smell your stinky roses. If you don't get it right, he'll run.

Closing the Funky Floodgates

For those of you who have tried everything but just can't stop swimming in your sweat, no worries. Dr. Novick says you should always talk to your dermatologist about the pros and cons of the following methods: prescription antiperspirants, oral medications, Botox, or surgery. Here she gives you the short version of how they work and why they may be the only way to make your whiff his gift!

Four Solutions to a Sweating Sweetie

- **The Rx.** "Prescription antiperspirants such as a commonly used product called Drysol work well. They can be irritating, though, to sensitive underarm skin," says Dr. Novick. There is no scent. They are applied at night to the underarm, feet, and hands. After nearly three days of use, many patients stop the sweats completely. Some women can even stop applying and reap the benefits of saying bye-bye to sweat for months.

- **The "Other" Pill.** "There are also oral medications that can be taken—such as glycopyrrolate—to inhibit sweating in the entire body. These are usually reserved for severe cases, since they have many unwanted side effects (dry mouth, blurred vision, and more)."

- **The Sweat Shot.** "It may seem drastic, but Botox is extremely safe and effective when used for extreme underarm sweating." Dr. Novick explains that Botox is injected superficially into the

underarm skin. Treatment with Botox can significantly min-
imize sweating for up to one year. Treatments typically cost
from $1,200 to $1,800. Some insurance plans will cover this
treatment.

- **The Sweat Surgery.** "Surgical removal of the sweat glands
of the underarms or splicing some of the nerves innervat-
ing the sweat glands can be performed in a certain subset of
patients. This is extreme." Dr. Novick says these procedures
are only used in limited circumstances (in patients who don't
have significant improvement from Botox or other treatments)
because of associated significant side effects like scarring and
compensatory hyperhidrosis (which means you sweat more
from other places because you can no longer sweat from your
armpits).

His Olfactory Odyssey Continues

So, you've got your body under stink control for the manly
stink patrol. But wait—there is one factor you may not have
factored in the smell wars. What about all that hot air you are
putting out there for him to hear and er…um…uh…smell?
Your breath, woman! That's another huge and fierce funky factor for him. If your breath speaks louder than your words, you
can kiss everyone kissable good-bye.

A popular and very good-looking TV chef talks about how
his relationship went sour. He had been dating a "smokin'"
Italian supermodel, adding, "She was a real Ferrari—tall, thin,
flawless, and fast." But when he kissed her, "She had the worst
breath ever!" He even tells how he tried incorporating mint or
parsley into his recipes in hopes of healing her halitosis. "Nothing worked," he said. "I had to break it off. I just couldn't fix
it." He needed a breath of fresh air.

It is reported that between 14 and 25 percent of Americans and 35 to 45 percent of the entire world's population has chronic bad breath. Market research shows that in 2007, Americans purchased nearly $9 billion in oral care products, from toothpaste and mouthwash to breath fresheners and floss, making kissing a billion-dollar business.

One of the country's top dentists, Dr. Terri Alani, says, "Many of these purchased items are completely ineffective, just mask the problem, or even make it worse. Especially if you are on a date and need to have the freshest breath possible. The odds and products are stacked against you." She explains that the net effect of alcohol-based mouthwashes on your breath is negative: "The alcohol dries your mouth, creating a great breeding ground for the kind of bacteria that contributes to bad breath." Instead, she suggests using mouthwashes with chlorine dioxide because it will attack most oral bacteria that causes the bad breath that keeps men running the other way while you run your mouth. It can keep your sassy breath fresh for up to eight hours. That's a lot of kissing or dissing him!

Dr. Alani says another trick for keeping fresh breath as part of your man plan is replacing your toothbrush every three to four months. Dr. Alani also suggests an inexpensive aide called a tongue scraper. She adds, "If you have white on your tongue, then you've got bacteria. You can either use a tongue scraper from your dentist's office or make sure you brush the middle third of your tongue for ten to fifteen strokes."

Dragon-Breath Diets

Dr. Alani explains that chronic bad breath can also be a product of your diet. "If you eat a lot of foods with high sulfur, such as onions, garlic, pastrami, and cabbage, or follow a low-carbohydrate diet, chances are your breath will be turning up any man's nose for good." For a quick food fix, Alani suggests puckering up to a slice of lemon right after a meal. If you can throw one in your handbag, go to the bathroom and give it a good suck or a little nosh. If he goes to the bathroom, try it quickly at the table. A lime also works if you are in a pinch. If the problem persists, seek help from the pros. Says Dr. Alani, "Your problem could be a plaque attack; a professional cleaning and gum screening are necessary."

Apparently, bacteria found on your tongue isn't the only thing that can cry foul from your mouth to your man. Other tongue-based date busters can speak for themselves. Dr. Alani says there are several different types of tongue troubles that can make a potential pucker go sour. These are the five on the tip of her tongue. Take care of them so you can move on with your sweet plan of conquering any man:

- **Fix Those Cranky Canker Sores.** Some of the causes of those unattractive-to-men menaces are simple: citrus fruits, stress, genetics, or biting your tongue. Dr. Alani suggests, "Avoid toothpastes with SLS [sodium lauvyl sulfate] and spicy or citrus foods. Gargle with saltwater solution or apply over-the-counter meds." They should go away in ten to fourteen days, and you should be ready to bust out that hot kissing machine again.

- **Stop Getting Hairy.** If your tongue is hairy or you find that it has dark brown or black on it, some of the causes could be coffee or tea; tobacco; antibiotics for bacterial infections (cold or fever); medicines for indigestion, such as Pepto-Bismol and Imodium, or a very dry mouth. Dr. Alani suggests that you brush your tongue twice a day and rinse with diluted hydrogen peroxide and water.

- **It's Not So Smooth to Be Pale and Smooth.** If your tongue looks pale or smooth, that's not a good move for you and your plan for a man. Some of the causes include iron-deficiency anemia, meaning your blood is lacking the oxygen-carrying capacity to keep tissue red. Dr. Alani suggests adding a little iron to your diet, and your iron man will be fast on his way to kissing you all day!

• **Oh No! Red Alert.** If your tongue is red and painful, you could be suffering from lack of B_3 (niacin) or B_{12} (folic acid). Then again it could also be caused by a "Big Red chewing gum attack." Cinnamon gum, mouthwash, or toothpaste, and acidic foods such as pineapples or tomatoes can also cause your tongue to be unkissable. Dr. Alani suggests adding vitamins to your diet and avoiding the list above. If you have to use that much gum to make your breath better, look out...he's already running.

• **Here Comes the Globe-Trotter Tongue.** If you have what dentists call a "geographic tongue," then your tongue probably looks like a map with protrusions and red patches, cracks, and crevices. He won't run the other direction because of this, but it is a little freaky if he gets up close and takes a gander. Some of the causes are genetics, stress, and high-sugar diets. So if you are aiming at perfection, Dr. Alani says to take some vitamin B and cut the sugar. You are sweet enough, baby!

You're the "Fresh-Maker"

Poof! You smell mahhhvelous. Now no man will sweat your sweetness. You've got the facts to get your "glisten and glow" on. You stopped the smelly sweat and put the bad breath to bed. All any man can do now is start sweatin' you. You'll leave him breathless and coming back for more.

five

The Vagina

Hey, Hey, Her Vajayjay!

Chuck and Robin had been dating for a few months. But this was the night Robin decided she was going to take their relationship a little further. They were spending a romantic night together: dinner, a wine bar, then back to Chuck's house for a nightcap and a little hookin' up. When the couple arrived at the house, Robin dipped in the bathroom to freshen up. She freshened her breath, her wrists and neck with a dab of perfume, and then realized maybe she should freshen up something else—her vajayjay.

She scanned the bathroom for supplies. Nothing. So she quickly folded a few squares of toilet paper, splashed a little warm water and hand soap on them, and gave her downtown a li'l scrub down. She then used more toilet paper to dry downtown. Now she felt a little more confident knowing that all was perfect in punani-land, or so she thought.

Chuck recalls that night: "We were kissing and carrying on. Then I put my hand downtown. I felt something strange."

37

Chuck then describes what is typically known as one of the most embarrassing moments in any woman's sexual exploits. "I asked her, 'Robin, are you having your period?'" Robin assured Chuck it wasn't her period, but Chuck insisted something foreign was in the small forest. Now both Chuck and Robin were foraging around downtown and through the woods, looking for something Chuck insisted wasn't supposed to be there.

Suddenly, Chuck pulled out a thin three-inch-long roll of white that (as he describes it) looked like a string. His reaction was, "Gross, Robin! What is this?" Her face turned bright red. She demanded the evidence. There it was—a spare square (or two) of toilet paper! Chuck describes the aftermath. "We both inspected it. Eww! What do you do after that? The mood was just gone. Plus, I kept thinking...What else does she have down there?"

His Main Focus

A woman's vagina is an area of her body that, when it comes to men, has very little wiggle room for mistakes. Men have an incredibly specific vision and expectation of what should be going on down there, even if they have no idea what really goes on down there. For some of you, this chapter will be information stored under the rubric "For Future Use Only." However, others will start their adventure before the final page is turned. Regardless, it is important to focus on some of the flaws men find here so that you feel completely comfortable with your experience—whenever it may be. Not everyone is ready to share that experience or special area with a man just yet, as it can make you feel vulnerable and emotionally exposed. A lot of thought should be a part of any decisions and plan when it comes to you, your vagina, and a man.

Why the Unswell Smell?

Dr. Christopher Jayne, one of the country's leading experts in women's sexual health, says that "despite their love for the vagina, most men are clueless when it comes to how it (and the other sexual organs) work." However, Dr. Jayne says that what men do know about women is very sensory oriented. "If a man complains about anything with a woman's sexual organs, it is usually how it tastes or smells. That said, a completely normal woman's taste and odor could be enjoyable to one and unpleasant to the next." But, as Dr. Jayne warns, if something isn't right down there, it is always unpleasant to *all*.

Even for healthy women, it is normal for vaginas to have bacteria in them. Dr. Jayne likens these "good" bacteria to the bacteria in other areas of the body, such as the digestive tract. These bacteria actually keep the body (and vagina) healthy and smelling good. However, if there is an infection or inflammation in the vagina, the normal bacteria can be overrun by an unhealthy type of bacteria or yeast. When this occurs, these unhealthy bacteria or yeast produce an unpleasant smell. Other infections related to sexually transmitted diseases can affect the smell of the vagina as well.

Dr. Jayne also says, "You are what you eat. After eating certain foods you may notice a change in your body's odor. The vagina is no different." He explains that spicy foods or foods with significant aromas, such as onions, garlic, curry, and Asian food, could alter the body's natural odors—including that of the vagina. "If you eat healthy, you smell healthy; if you eat junky, you smell junky." Besides foods, tobacco and other drugs can cause the vagina to have a bitter taste and pungent odor even with the normal or "good bacteria" flourishing. Beer is tantamount to drinking yeast straight up, so if you want to keep it clean, pour out the yeastier alcoholic drinks like beer and wine and stick to the hard alcohols (of course, in moderation).

Unfortunately, for most women, vaginal odors are not related to food, drinks, tobacco, or sexually transmitted diseases. They are caused by either a yeast infection or a bacterial infection. "If you are overly zealous about keeping that area clean (that is, douching), you can, in some cases, actually produce more odors," Dr. Jayne cautions. He explains that when the normal environment of the vagina has been altered, the good bacteria naturally produced by the body decreases. This could cause an increase in concentrations of either yeast or bad bacteria. When this occurs, it affects the balance, or pH, of the vagina. (The pH is how acidic or basic something is. The higher the number, the more basic something is; the lower the number, the more acidic something is. A pH of 7 is neutral.)

The pH of a normal vagina is generally in the 4 to 5 range (more acidic). When you remove the good bacteria by over-cleaning the vagina, you make the environment more basic, which could lead to a yeast infection and odor. Dr. Jayne says your physician will normally treat this by lowering the pH of the vagina (back to normal) and increasing the concentrations of good bacteria.

He says that as a general rule, women should not douche. If you are going to freshen up without creating embarrassing situations such as Robin's toilet paper incident, Dr. Jayne recommends using products only externally, such as soap and water or feminine wipes. These wipes are produced by the same companies that make the douches you see on the market (Massengill and Playtex) but are only used on the outside areas of the vagina, so they don't generally cause problems. The wipes can actually be quite a good little secret weapon in the war against vajayjay odor. Because they come in individual packets (like the kind you get at a BBQ restaurant for your hands), they can be discreetly carried around with you—even in the smallest of handbags.

Grooming: Going Risqué with a Risk

Most women know the majority of men prefer women to be well groomed to the point of perfection, whether it's a Brazilian bikini wax or the famed "landing strip." But when it comes to going bare down there, as one man said, "No way. You only know it's okay to play when there is a little grass on the infield." Another man admitted, "I dated a girl who shaved everything but left a mini horse's mane. That didn't work well because I had braces." And then there's the man who said this: "There's nothing worse when you're in the middle of that sexy moment, you get to slip her out of her underwear and, *wow*, out pops a giant Nerf ball. Nerf balls were fun to play with when we were kids. Grown-up guys don't like them so much." Men, aren't they so eloquent?

Speaking of lady grooming, according to doctors, there are no real health benefits to keeping the hair down there cut short, shaved, waxed, or lasered. If anything, many say the more you do downtown, the more likely you are to have a problem. "The hair protects you against infection. In addition, it helps keep the pH balance at the natural level," Dr. Jayne says. Clipping, cutting, and waxing can put you at risk for skin irritations and skin infections, even when executed correctly and in a sterile environment.

While on the topic of grooming, this next lesson is a short one, with no gray areas. When a woman named Betty Saxe was getting a divorce, her husband left her with this: "By the way, Betty, in my new future, I hope to never see another gray hair down there." He pointed at her punani! It was just enough to make a divorced woman turn into a determined woman. That's how Betty Saxe came up with a product called Priva'tone. Her product is a formula of dye that she says has been tested by dermatologists and is safe (as the product's website says) for "hair in your private areas." Betty adds that her dye comes in black and brown, is applied using a brush similar to a mascara wand, can be used on sensitive skin, takes only eight to ten minutes to work, and is even popular with men!

Smell-Tale Signs

Finally, an all points bulletin with this next information should go out to every woman in the dating trenches. It is what men call "the swipe and sniff test." When a man wants to know what you smell like before he decides to go downtown for a little pleasure, he apparently performs this test with amazing alacrity and adeptness. It goes something like this:

- **The Lure.** He kisses you.

- **The Swipe.** He sneaks a finger or two around your downtown for a sampling.

- **The Distraction.** He puts his arms around you and begins to kiss your neck.

- **The Smell.** His arms are wrapped around your neck; you are in ecstasy and don't notice that he only wrapped his arms around you so that he can covertly smell the fingers he just took a sampling with.

This test is performed with such perfection you would think they were taught it at birth. So, ladies, if you've been out dancing or had a long day at work, in the gym, or outside, just know that wiping it before he's swiping it will keep you from wiping out!

Planning for a Later Date

Now that you know how to handle your hygiene so that he will respond the way you want, relax. Enjoy a few moments of basking in your bold and beautiful self—you deserve it. But if you decide to keep this information to yourself and use it on him at a later date, then you have every right to wait and master the other facets of your man plan. Your vagina isn't going anywhere and neither will he if you decide to pick up the plan later in life, when you are most comfortable and know it is right for you.

six

Body Hair
Shaving Your Way Out
of a Hairy Situation

As Josh describes her, Renee was a young, vibrant, and breathtaking Italian woman. She had long raven hair, flawless olive skin, full lips, and a set of hips that could put a guy like Josh into Frederick's of Hollywood fantasyland in an instant. Josh and Renee had been dating for three months, but it was not until the day he decided to pop by Renee's house for a little unexpected visit that he really got to know her.

The front door was open, so he let himself in. What he saw next was hair-raising. Renee was in the bathroom with her face covered in a white creamy substance. The source of that substance was held in one hand as the other adeptly spread the substance over her neck. Renee, startled to see Josh, quickly grabbed a towel. She told Josh her skin was feeling dry, so she was trying out a new face mask. But it was too late for excuses. Josh had already seen the evidence and unmasked the mystery. Renee had tried to slip it away in her embarrassment, but Josh had caught her "Nair"-handedly.

Josh says he and Renee soon parted ways, and Renee moved on. But after Josh, there was Cody, then John, then Reggie and Billy. Renee had more hair than any man could bear—hair on her chin, lip, neck, arms. After years of getting caught in nearly every act of waxing, shaving, tweezing, plucking, bleaching, lasering, and, yes, "Nairing," Renee had nearly given up on love, until she found Stephen. Stephen didn't care about all that hair. He had it, too.

Let's Face It...

Men aren't keen on your body hair. They want your skin to be silky smooth like you were a baby and never grew up! On your head...now that is different. Every woman has hair and struggles with keeping all ends groomed. Men don't want anything to do with that struggle. They don't want to know about it or see it...ever. They just want to reach over to touch you and know that you have no body hair.

If you haven't found a date that is your hair mate, there are a few things to know about how to get it not to grow. Enlisted for this troublesome task is Dr. Ken Hollis, an über-smart skin doc specializing in dermal surgery. When it comes to the face, Dr. Hollis says there are four traditional ways to remove unwanted hair: bleaching, waxing, shaving, and using a laser. When picking the procedure you are most comfortable with, you should also consider the area on the body you are working on. Each area has some specific requirements and shortcomings when it comes to hair removal. Getting the right combo can be key. Your facial hair acts differently than your arm hair, which even acts differently than your armpit hair.

Underarm Hair

When considering ways to get rid of unwanted armpit hair, waxing may not be your best choice, according to Dr. Hollis. "Waxing may cause redness, as it is a sensitive area." You may just plan on relying on the razor. If he catches you a little on the hairy side in this area, there is very little forgiveness. That's just plain gross in his world. So get a good razor and get to it.

For a good armpit shave, Dr. Hollis recommends using a dual-sided razor, shaving in the direction of hair growth and moisturizing during and after. "Don't use soap—only shaving creams or gels. Pick products that have moisturizing agents."

If shaving and waxing aren't your thing, then go-go gadget laser. Dr. Hollis says the hair under there is stubborn but will say bye-bye with a little help from the laser. A note of caution: "You shouldn't wear deodorants/antiperspirants while you are going through the laser procedure. The area needs to be perfectly clean or it will irritate the skin. Just stick to lotion for two to three days after treatment," advises Dr. Hollis. Therefore, if you tend to have a little stink to your sweat, then try this procedure when you won't be seeing him for a few days.

Arm Hair

Waxing your arm hair is an option, but not if you have sensitive skin, Dr. Hollis says. Also, for those of you sensitive types out there, you should just say no to the Nair type of hair-removal products, as they may irritate sensitive skin. Take a test ride first. Extremely hairy arms, especially those with darker hair, can be a major turnoff, but if you have a manageable amount of arm hair or lighter colored hair, this won't be an issue for most men.

If you plan on shaving off your arm hair, you'd better be ready to keep on shaving. No man thinks stubble is subtle. You will have to maintain this on a regular basis or it will lead to major stubble, says Dr. Hollis. However, the best way to get rid of that annoying arm hair is the laser, but only if you have light skin and dark hair, says Dr. Hollis.

Leg Hair

The upper half of you is important to a man, but traditionally your legs can kick his interest up a notch. When the legs do the talkin', he'll come a-walkin'. So who better to turn to for advice on legging up the competition than a dynamic dancing duo—twin sisters Kimberly and Katherine Corp, former Rockettes and owners of Pilates on Fifth, a Pilates studio in midtown Manhattan.

If you're thinking of waxing, according to Kimberly, "Know your skin type and your hair type: Are you thin-skinned or thick-skinned? Sensitive or tough? Is your hair light or dark?" If your skin is sensitive, then waxing is not for you! If you consider yourself Ms. Thick Skin, or have darker hair, you may prefer waxing.

If you are going to go the razor route and want the closest shave, there is an amazing way to get the best shave, according to Kimberly and Katherine: "Shave with cold water *before* your shower or bath." The hot water of your shower/bath makes your legs swell just enough to prevent the closest shave possible. Thus, try shaving your legs sitting on the edge of the bathtub using cold water . . . as cold as you can stand it. You'll get a much closer shave, and your shave will last longer!

Kimberly warns, "If you have sensitive skin, it is best *not* to exfoliate before shaving. When you moisturize, use something gentle and not laden with fragrances, which can cause irritation." Loofahs should also be used on the days you are not shaving.

The knee can make or break the leg. If you notice your knees looking a little flaky or gray and ashy, he will, too. For extremely dry skin (especially around the knees and ankles), mix your favorite lotion with oil (half lotion, half baby oil or any other skin oil), shake it, and apply it as you normally would all over the leg. Another good tip: if you have a favorite scented lotion and it has corresponding bath oil, mix them together (half scented lotion/half bath oil). This makes for a mean combination: sweet smell and soft skin.

Even if your knees are beautifully smooth, flaws do find their way. Kimberly jokes, "For twin sisters who were both Rockettes, we found ways to accidentally knick up our legs that you wouldn't even think existed." But the two also found ways to cover them up: "If you have a bruise you're trying to hide—or a birthmark—nothing works better than good ole makeup." Don't bother with expensive makeup for a bruise on your leg! Any drugstore brand should suffice. Also, if you have cut yourself shaving, a nice tiny Band-Aid will be much better than makeup!

Another way to win with your legs is to tap into a tan (without the sun). Kimberly says your legs will always be more appealing to men if they have a little healthy and tan-toned look to them. There are some great spray-on products, as well as lotions with shimmer or gold and tan tones that do the trick. But she warns not to overdo it; you can sparkle your way into stripperville if you aren't careful. Traditional tanning creams and sprays can smell awful or look orange, but one option is to go with the gradual glow. New lotions that promise a tempered type of tan that grows darker with each application are the way to go. These types of lotions are great on the legs because they don't cause staining on the knee, toe, or ankle regions; instead, you get a nice even tan without the major stink factor. The goal isn't Ms. Oompa-Loompa; it is Ms. Sexy St. Tropez.

She's Smooth and Slick!

After taking care of all the hair up there and getting down to the hairy situation below, you are now ready for a killer attack. You should be on point with your "stems" (as men like to call them). Your legs are toned, tanned, shaven, shimmered, and shaped. You've perfected the pair even down to the hair. So, if he has even a single complaint, then show no restraint— kick him to the curb, Rockette style!

seven

Head Hair

Wash Your "Fajita Hair"

On their second date, Blaine, a debonair dilettante of sorts, took Jessica, a self-proclaimed conservative perfectionist, to dinner at his favorite Mexican restaurant. He had a plan. The restaurant was known for its super-size margaritas, which were rumored to be made with a splash of Everclear. "I know this is horrible," Blaine says, joking, "but on our first date, Jessica was way too stiff. But she was too hot to dump. So I figured we'd get a little loopy on the liquor and see if it got any better." Blaine ordered margaritas for the table, and with them the other thing the restaurant was known for, its fajitas: an entrée that came to the table steaming and sizzling, a perfect complement to the Big Gulp–style margaritas.

Three margaritas later, the two were hitting it off, but the bliss was short-lived. Jessica ended up back at Blaine's bachelor pad. After about fifteen minutes of making out, Blaine called her a cab. But why? "I was kissing the back of her neck, and her hair smelled like she hadn't washed it since birth!" he explains.

"It was a blend of BO like she'd been to the gym. Total buzz-kill." Blaine was right. Jessica's hair did stink of BO—bell peppers and onions, that is! The fabulous fajitas from their magical Mexican fiesta had sizzled and steamed their way right into her roots. She was another innocent victim of the dreaded "fajita head." It seemed all that sizzle had caused her date's attraction to fizzle.

Rounding Up the Usual Smell-spects

This hairy phenomenon is not limited to just the fajita. Of course there are a myriad of other culprits, including greasy diners (where frying fills the air, soaking the hair), smoky bars, coffeehouses, sweaty dance clubs, sweaty gyms, and any barbecue establishment or outdoor-grilling gathering. No busy woman could possibly wash her hair after all of the above, but no man wants to smell any of the above in her hair. Your hair absorbs more smells and gives off more smells then most of your body. If that smell is bad, then that can defeat any strong perfume, lotion, or body wash you may be using to cover it up. No woman can be fresh out of the shower always, but there are a few tricks to keeping the fajitas and coffeehouses out of your hair before his attraction for you stops sizzlin' and starts fizzlin'.

Someone who knows a lot about fajita hair and has been in the business of beauty for years is salon owner Rachel Gower of the Upper Hand Salon in Houston, Texas—aka Fajita Central. Rachel laughs. "I am one of those people who actually schedules visits to my favorite Tex-Mex restaurant around my hair-washing schedule," she says. "I cannot stand fajita hair." Therefore, instead of letting it get to your head, Rachel has a few "heady" solutions to combat the stinky and, as the saying goes, "wash that man-burger right out of your hair."

Rachel knows the pros (and cons) of using that time-honored traditional approach to the no-wash hair—baby powder. "Back in the day, baby powder was the only option and not a particularly great one at that," she explains. According to Rachel, talc or starch, the active ingredients in baby powder, are the most effective way to absorb oil and neutralize odor. "Let's face it, if the talc and light fragrance found in most baby powders can combat *that* odor, it should be able to handle fajita and StairMaster hair."

Problems, however, abound. Rachel explains that besides the obvious and inevitable mess that will surely ensue, powder on the scalp can lead to self-imposed dandruff. "When an oily scalp is fed dry powder, clumping is likely to occur."

No Man Wants to Date a Flake

Rachel says that an alternative solution is a dry shampoo (shampooing sans water). Often times these dry solutions are called dry powders. They are the fastest way to make your hair man-friendly and keep you feeling fabulous, fajita or not. Not only will an aerosol dry shampoo or hair powder absorb oil and neutralize odor, but it will also provide maximum volume and grip (great for creating a Brigitte Bardot updo).

"These products are fabulously helpful," Rachel says, "but be careful; if you use too much, unless you're platinum blond, you could end up with a chalky white halo." Every man wants an angel, but a chalky white halo is a no-go. Have no fear. To solve this problem, several companies have concocted dry shampoos or hair powders with tint (black, brown, red, and dirty blond). Available in loose powder or in aerosol form, the tinted dry shampoos also allow a bit of cheating between color appointments. Ha! Now you can trick your smell and your gray hair or brown roots. He'll never get to the root of that! Rachel

believes you should experiment with different brands to find
the best product for you, but dry shampoo of any brand or
color is a must-have for vanity counters in every home. Many
come in travel sizes, too, so throw that mini magical powder
into your bag before you cruise on out to meet your man. If
you have a fajita or coffee date, before you exit the restaurant
or coffeehouse, run to the restroom and give your hair a little
spray.

Another option is a little more involved but a great prep step in
a pinch. You can create your own refreshing hair tonic, or what
they call in the industry "prep spray." According to the experts,
tea tree oil is widely known as an effective and natural antiseptic,
but it can also work nicely as an odor neutralizer. Most professional hair-care lines have a good prep spray that acts as a foundation for additional styling products. Because prep sprays are
usually very light in texture and fragrance in addition to being
oil free, they make great refreshers, according to Rachel.

She advises that you find a hair prep product with a subtle
fragrance that makes his heart sing and then make it your own
by adding eight to ten drops of tea tree oil (per eight ounces
of solution). Once you create your tonic, bottle it. Then strategically locate it where you'll need it most (home, gym, boyfriend's house, or travel bag). You won't have to waste time
washing your hair. Instead you can enjoy him more and he'll
enjoy your scent to the max.

Prep So You Can Skip a Step

But that is only the first step. "It is still better than having to
wash and dry your whole head of hair," Rachel says, "but you
will absolutely need to put a bit of effort into this! Spray alone
is only half of the job." Apparently your tonic will neutralize
odor, freshen your hair, and reactivate your styling product, but

you need to finish the job with a high-quality professional hair dryer, a diffuser, and/or a natural-boar-bristle brush. "Round-brush your locks back into shape." Rachel also says that if you decide to go a different direction and walk a little on the wild side (and spend less time on the consuming side), then you can also use your homemade prep spray to create a tousled carefree and casual look. Be creative with your coif. Men love it when you feel sexy about yourself. A carefree look is what they want, even if it took a lot of care to get you there!

If you are really pressed for time, Rachel says you can try using your favorite fabric freshener (such as Febreze). Who knew it made such an effective hair and scalp deodorizer? She cautions that those with damaged hair or sensitive scalps should proceed with a bit of trepidation and test a patch before going for it. But she believes you can certainly brush up a hairy situation with a mountainy fresh fragrance. If you are at his house and find nothing else, it is better than bustin' out with bad-smelling hair.

You Aren't Fooling the Foul

While touting freshening fragrances in this instance is a good thing, Rachel says, there are ways to blow it. Into the category of "people think that it works, but it really doesn't" fall the following:

- **Perfume.** This is the equivalent of adding insult to injury in the world of smelly hair. Not only are you mottling the intended aroma, but the additional oil you're usually adding will only compound the gunk-magnet effect.

- **Heat.** Applying heat to an already ripe situation will certainly aggravate it. Think in terms of applying heat to an injury. In addition, you are effectively giving the stinkiness a life of its own (legs, if you will). The same holds true for curling irons and flat irons.

- **Steam Rooms or Steamy Bathrooms.** When you've reached this point in your quest, it's probably easier to just give in and wash your hair. If you want to use steam, slather on a decadent damage-repair mask and then steam away. In fact, many salons use steamers to give incredible deep treatments. Use your shower at home to create a similar effect, but don't stand in there and wave your hair around hoping you will dissipate the doughnut smell. Just shower and get rid of the grunge.

Hair That Sizzles

Finally, when it comes to the man who you know is finicky about fajita hair, one way to really avoid the aforementioned sizzle-then-fizzle effect (such as the one experienced by Blaine due to Jessica's hair) is to instruct all members of the restaurant's waitstaff not to deliver—under any circumstances—steaming and sizzling fajitas to your table or to any other table within a fifteen-foot radius. It sounds a bit challenging, but it's been accomplished. But the best advice is to stick with the slick and easy ways to avoid a "funk-a-fried 'fro."

GET READY

Blushing About Cosmetics and Beauty

eight

Makeup

Punched in the Eye or Smoky Eye?

While out with his guy friends one night, Chad—a suave-looking, smooth-talking serial dater and notorious modelizer—met Ardriana, a hot Brazilian model. He got her number, waited a few days, then called and asked her to lunch. "When I am out at night and meet an attractive woman, before I decide to take her home (or even ask her out for dinner), no matter how hot I think she is, I wait a day and instead meet her for lunch." The two met for lunch. Chad noticed she didn't speak great English, and his Portuguese was rusty. "Language wasn't the issue; a man can always work through the language barrier." But there was another barrier that seemed impenetrable to Chad. "Her makeup was so heavy, it was weighing me down—and I wasn't even wearing it! I could just picture all that makeup getting on my face after we kissed, my shirts after we hugged, and all over my bed after she came home with me."

Ahhh...so this is how Chad came up with his take-a-woman-to-lunch-then-decide-if-you-want-to-date-her theory. "You may meet her at night where the lights are low, but hold out until you can see her for real. Women always look worse in the daylight." Chad continues with a litany of fatal makeup flaws that would make even Tammy Faye Bakker bat an eye. "Women are still wearing too much caked-on, baked-on makeup. During the day, you can see how much they are trying to cover up by how much #%@ they put on! My friends and I just want to hand them a washcloth and a giant bar of soap and say, 'Rub-a-dub.'"

His Look, Your (Right) Hook

No matter what Chad says, it is never a bad time to perfect your look so that you can give him the hook the next time he makes fun of your makeup (daylight notwithstanding). Men everywhere say they like a more natural look on a woman. Anytime they can see your makeup, whether it is on your face or their sheets, they feel you must have too much on. This of course doesn't mean you shouldn't wear any. If they saw you without any, they would say you looked plain and tired. But because they really don't know what goes into that natural look of yours, you can pull off an effortless look with your own bag of natural makeup tricks. One man who has revolutionized the cosmetics industry based on theories like this is John Demsey, the president of Estée Lauder. John puts it best when he says, "It takes a whole lot of makeup to look like you aren't wearing any makeup!" John recommended two amazing experts to help women know exactly what men want when it comes to makeup. Enlisted for this makeover are celebrity makeup artists Gregory Arlt and Linda Hay.

Gregory has nearly twenty years in the field and has glammed up some of the most glamorous of red-carpet walkers, including Victoria Beckham and Mary J. Blige. Linda's twenty years in the business has been spent making the most perfect women in the world look even more perfect, including Gisele Bundchen and Heidi Klum. Linda has some encouraging information to start this makeup makeover with: "No matter how perfect the models I work with may seem, I still have to use a lot of makeup on them (sometimes full-body makeup). But I've found a way to make it all look natural. No man would ever even know."

Gregory agrees with Linda about the amount of makeup it takes to get the look you want for a magazine *or* a man. "It may take seven eye shadows to get one natural-looking lid." But he warns about overdoing it. "Makeup is not an accessory. Men don't understand all the goop hanging from your face. Ladies, you want your skin to look expensive and young; think dewy, not gooey!"

Two-Faced Is Fabulous for Makeup and Men

There are two looks that need to be perfected when it comes to makeup and cosmetics and men. Your plan should include a day look and a night look. A third plan may be necessary, once you read your man a little, but the first two are imperative.

Making Your Day Face

Most men don't know what to tell you if you are doing something they don't like with your makeup (like wearing too much base or blush), because they don't know the terminology. But they do have their own "made-up makeup" language. When it comes to what they think looks beautiful on you in the day, they say things like, "She needs to look fresh, clean, wholesome, youthful, washed, and dewy." Pay attention to these words. This is how men communicate the look they want. Now, to translate the look from their lips to yours, Linda and Gregory show you six simple steps to get that fresh face without a trace of makeup (or at least none he can see):

• **Exfoliate.** For sexy, touchable skin, you need an even surface to start with.

• **Coverage.** Blend all the way from your hairline to your collarbone—no exceptions. Make sure you allow your moisturizer or foundation time to settle and dry. If you don't, your bronzer and blush will go on splotchy. Also, stay away from powder products. Go instead with the yummy dewy creams. If you have no flaws (sun spots, scars), use a "gradual-glow" self-tanner (for the face). If you have a few flaws, use your favorite tinted moisturizer (one with an SPF is best). In addition, use a good liquid concealer to hide the smaller flaws, hyperpigmentation, or blemishes. If you have a lot of flaws, use oil-free liquid foundation. Avoid powders, cream powders, and pressed powders. If you feel like you are having an oil-slick moment, then lightly dust a hint of translucent mineral powder in your T zone. A light dust, not a crop dusting!

• **Bronzer.** Dust across cheek, near hairline, around chin, across the bridge of your nose. Look for warm golden colors, not too orange. Make sure there is a little shimmer, not a sparkle.

• **Blush.** Choose a pinkish color (peachy for darker skin) and put just a little dot of color at the top of the apple of your cheek (not too much or you'll look like a Raggedy Ann doll). Don't fill it in; rather, leave it the same way you would see your cheeks when they get a sweet little kiss from the sun. If you want an even fresher look, use a cream blush or a cheek tint. But be careful with the tint; when you put it on, it's not going anywhere anytime soon, so pick the right spot and get cheeky with your new sun-kissed look.

• **Lips.** Use a lip stain or longer-wearing lip colors (also called indelible lipsticks) that are a small bump up from your natural pink lips. Dab a hint of light gloss. To perfect your pout, you need to keep those luscious lips hydrated, even if it is just Chap-

Stick you are smoothing on. If you feel you need more volume and must use a lip pencil, choose one that is a shade slightly darker than your natural lips. Outline the lips at the very tip of your natural lip line; keep the line smudgy, so that it looks smoldering. Caution: Don't paint too far outside the lines or you will look like the Joker; plus, it ages you.

- **Eyes.** They tell the whole story. Use a light liquid concealer around eyes (for extra help carrying all your bags!). Then mascara on the top and bottom lashes. Make sure you replace your mascara every three months or so as bacteria builds up quickly. Make sure your mascara is evenly distributed to avoid larger and flaky-looking clumps. Lashes should always look effortlessly feathery and lush. *Important:* Always curl your lashes before applying mascara. Don't bother with gimmicky heated curlers; just use the one your mother and her mother used before you. If you absolutely feel naked in the day without your eye shadows, you are officially allowed to pick one (only one) light, natural-looking shadow to put all over the lid from brow to lash. Limit the amount of shimmer and sparkle. Let your eyes do the sparklin'.

Your Sunset Sparkle

Now that the day look has been achieved, it is time for Linda and Gregory to move on to the second look that men like. Your night look. Linda says, "You never want your night look to be too far off from your day look; it confuses men. You need to add some drama, but don't think you need to add too much to get that drama." When asked how women should look when they are going out at night, men responded with words like "sultry," "mysterious," "sexy," "bedroom eyes," "sensuous," and "kissable." Knowing this, Linda and Gregory say it's time to pump up the makeup menu by adding some "side dishes" to the already made-up day face.

• **Night Eyes.** Linda's choice: soft smoky eye. The traditional smoky eye is generally black, but you can sass up the eyes by using a dark brown, plum, chocolate, or gray. The perfect smoky eye starts with lining the lid from the inside corner to the outside corner. Use that same eye pencil to line the bottom lash line. Now it is time to soften and smudge. Take a similar-colored shadow (matching the eye pencil) and smudge it in with the lines on the lower and upper lids. This will set the pencil and create a soft and out-of-focus phenomenon. Last, take the same shadow you used to smudge the liner with (or another similar shade) and lead the eye upward with the shadow. How far should you take it? If you have smaller eyes, keep it soft and take the shadow up, further away from the eye, past the crease and above. If you have larger eyes, just smudge up the shadow a smidgen. Keep it mostly close to the lash line.

Gregory's choice: bright lights, night city. If you just aren't feelin' the smoky eye, well, brighten up—literally. Men love gold in your eyes. If you are thirty-seven or older, you should forget the frosts and eliminate the extreme shimmers. They can settle into the fine lines and actually highlight your wrinkles. If you still want that bright eye, use brighter-colored satiny-looking shadows with just a hint of sheen in them. *Important:* No matter what age you are, never go with matte on the eyes or lips; it just looks flat, lifeless, and boring.

• **Nighttime Lip Service.** When the sun goes down, Linda and Gregory know a lot of women in Tinseltown that want to up the ante by going with darker shades of lipsticks or an alarming fire-engine red. "Ladies, it's time to put out the fire," Gregory says, to which Linda adds, "Men are typically frightened by dark or bright red lipsticks. They get intimidated by the amount of 'foreign color' on your lips." Apparently, men want lips the way they came, soft and puckering pink. "Plus,"

Gregory says, "when they see extremely dark or a mod type of makeup, they think 'Dracula lips.'" Big take-home here: Think kissable lips, not bloodthirsty ones.

Please Don't "Makeup" My Bed

Now that you have a plan for looking your best day and night, it is time for a little after-hours party. If you are planning on sleeping over, you will need a plan for your makeup. He may want you to leave his bed made up, but he will never want you to leave it with makeup. Men complain all the time about women getting makeup on their towels, washcloths, sheets, and pillowcases.

Gregory suggests carrying around a few makeup wipes in your handbag. He says the official order of takeoff should start with the lips and eyes, "but you better save some of that wipe to dust over your face in hopes of picking up what's left over." Gregory also says that if you need a li'l test to see if what you've got on is going to rub off on his sheets or towels, then use toilet paper and do a quick check of your own.

However, if you just can't do without your Tammy Faye face when you stay at his place, then you need to replace a few of your faves. Linda and Gregory suggest the following as products that promise not to tick him off by rubbing off:

- Loose mineral foundation—If you have to have some coverage, it doesn't transfer.

- Lip tint/stain—You can use this on lips and cheeks for an evening glow that won't go.

- ChapStick/lip balm or some type of moisturizing lip treatment.

Porn-Star Pretty?

While on the subject of makeup for shackin' up, a certain look comes to mind. In the world of men, there is always a group who occasionally like their women to look a little less wholesome and a lot more like a...well...porn star. This select group of men will admit that if a woman he liked really met a fantasy of his (at least once every few months), he would fall head over heels for her. This may be out of the question to you, but at least you'll know what to do if one day you decide to go with the third plan—the porn-star plan. The celebrity that has perfected that porn-star look is Pam Anderson. As her makeup artist, Gregory's got the scoop on said goop: "With Pamela, it's picture-perfect porn." So how about a look at the recipe for your man's *Baywatch* fantasy?

Pamela Anderson's Porn-Pretty Makeup

- Smoky black or dark blue eye pencil lining eyes from inside corner to outside corner and lining bottom lids.

- Black liquid eyeliner for a thicker lash line on the top lid.

- Black or dark blue shadow

- Bronzer everywhere (highlights top of breasts for an extra li'l oomph!)

- Frosty pale pink, thick, sticky, gooey goddess gloss

- Lashes galore! "Oh, you bet she piles those lashes on in a fabulous fashion," Gregory says.

"Makeup" Your Future with Him

So no matter which look you choose, from a fresh face to the porn plan, you've now got the looks to keep him lookin' your way every day. Any man will swoon at your fresh day face because it looks effortless and stunning. He will also go wild over your sultry night face and how you managed to avoid leaving it behind on his pillow! Plus, now you know how to make him sweat if he has a fantasy he wants met. All of that is the kind of stuff you just can't make up.

nine

Perfume
Chanel No. 5, Gas Mask Included

David and Sophia had been hanging out for a few months. During those few months, David would make inquiries to Sophia, like, "Is that rose lotion you have on?" or "You smell like red roses; is that your perfume?" Once, when she was cold, he let her borrow his scarf. Upon returning it, he text-messaged her, "I can smell your roses around my neck on my scarf." Sophia was thrilled! Her scent was wrapped around his neck and wafting upward, reminding him of her. However, Sophia may have been seeing David's scent scenario through her own rose-colored lenses. David's side of the scent story wasn't so sweet.

He explains, "Yeah, I could smell Sophia's scent of roses around my neck on my scarf. It was wrapped around my neck, choking me with roses. I got the worst headache." The next time Sophia slept at David's, she poured on the rose perfume, thinking it would pour on his sweet side. Plus, she could leave a little of her scent between his sheets for him to sleep on the next night. When David awoke the next morning, he recalls, "I had another horrible headache. Her scent was making me sick. It was so strong, it was strangling me." Not only did David not like the scent of roses, but it reminded him of something that wasn't sexy. "My grandmother used to wear rosewater perfume. Every time she came over on holidays she would leave a trail of roses, which was sweet when I was a kid. But now?! My girlfriend and my grandma shouldn't smell the same!"

David finally told Sophia, but it was too late; the relationship had already started to stink! Sophia thought all along she was doing things right because David was always inquiring about her perfume. David thought he was doing things right by asking about it because that meant he didn't like it. "Men don't want to have a scent popping out and slapping them in the face every time they see you. They want to get up close to you and smell it, like they are the only ones in the world who get to know that smell because they are so close to you." He continues, "If men are asking questions about your scent, it isn't because they like it; it is probably because it is too strong—or too wrong."

A Diddy on Smelling Sexy

Sean "Diddy" Combs knows just how to pick a fragrance for women that dances with a man's senses, lingers, and then leaves him wanting more. Not only is he a celebrated icon in the hip-hop industry, but he also has a successful clothing line and one of the top-selling female fragrances in the country: Unforgivable Woman. "I have a true understanding of women...the power of fragrance is the ultimate tool in the art of seduction. A woman can easily use the power of fragrance in her 'Man Plan.'" Combs believes every woman should have her signature scent, adding, "It should be defining and capture her unique essence." But he warns of moderation. "A woman's fragrance should be worn delicately, lightly on the neck, behind the ears, so those close to her will be able to subtly notice it."

Therefore, when it comes to leaving a little lingering part of you for him to smell, remember that subtlety can go a long way where a man's nose is concerned. Combs explains, "There is nothing sexier than catching a trace of your lover's scent on your collar, your T-shirt... or better yet your sheets."

Again and again—from P. Diddy and Paris, France, to Paris, Texas—droves of men have described just what it takes to seduce them with your scent, yet despite the fabled notoriety of various overscented scenarios, droves of women continue to douse on dumbfounding doses. Adam, a serial dater and lover of all things women, says, "No matter how hot a woman is, if her perfume reaches you before you reach her, you generally want to reach out for a gas mask!" Lee, another fed-up nose, sums it up by saying, "There can be a right perfume but not a wrong perfume—unless it's way too strong. That's all wrong." Plus, when your perfume is too loud, men say, it says all the wrong things about you. "If it's too strong, it can make a woman unattractive," Brandon admits. Finally, another bachelor named Bill blurts out this beauty: "I don't need her broadcasting her perfume for the benefit of the entire roomful of people. Just for me... all for me."

The Smelly Crime Scene

Their smellers (and egos) seem super-sensitive, almost to a fault, but as witnessed, it also seems your scent may have the power to overpower a man in a fatal way. It's time to teach your scent to stretch its fragrant tentacles across the room and tantalize rather than terrorize. So how do you keep your favorite fragrance from claiming any more victims?

Carolyn Griffin—perfume biographer, aficionado, and creator

of Scent Signals, a website dedicated to perfume—has been study-ing the delicious or deleterious effects of scents for more than two decades. Carolyn concedes that wearing too much, too strong, too soon is what men typically notice up front. But that's just a whiff of the way scents affect a man. She believes that if women realize the real power scent can spray over a man, they will be able to harness an amazing, mesmerizing effect over them.

Carolyn begins the enchanting lesson in the grocery store, with a stop in the produce and spice department. "The Smell and Taste Treatment and Research Foundation in Chicago has discovered that wearing spicy floral perfumes can make men think you are pounds lighter than you really are." And she adds, "According to the same research, the smell of grapefruit can make men put your age at years younger than you actually are."

Carolyn says, "The Smell and Taste Treatment and Research Foundation also discovered that men are aroused by the combined scents of pumpkin pie and lavender." Their tests showed the smell of cinnamon buns appeals to men as well. "So if you're planning a romantic evening, spray your sheets with a little lavender water and burn candles scented as pumpkin pie or cinnamon."

A few drops of essential oil in a romantic bath followed by a sensuous massage can also crank his engine. Try adding a few drops of jasmine or ylang-ylang oil to your bathwater and rich unscented oil. "There's a reason why some cultures wouldn't let their virgins near these obviously sexual white flowers," says Carolyn. Vanilla also seems to soothe and comfort both men and women, and is a good choice as a candle or massage lotion.

Get the Smell Away from Him

Are there perfume scents men absolutely hate? It seems a good rule of thumb to go by is his history. "If he's had a really bad experience associated with certain notes (perfume base smells), or associates scents with his mother, grandmother, or schoolteacher, you should choose again!" She adds, "My coworker Jeff had a bottle of floral perfume dumped on his head by a bratty girl when he was boy. To this day, he hates floral perfumes," says Carolyn.

She also explains one good rule of thumb. "If you steer clear of things your mother or grandmother would have worn, like roses or gardenias or those old-school perfumes like Shalimar or Lauren, et cetera, you can bet you're on the right scent trail to luring him in." (And while it can be sexy to leave behind a hint of your scent—a subtle trace on his pillows and sheets can drive him wild and keep him thinking of you—don't expect him to be pleased to find your perfume on his car seats or sofa, as that can feel invasive.)

The fact is that most men don't know the names of the scents they like the most—they just know they like them. You can ask them if they are musk men or more into cedar and bergamot, but you'll usually get a blank stare in response. Instead, Carolyn recommends exploring and playing with scents together with your man.

All of this magic can be tragic if you pour on too much of your potion. If a woman wears the same scent for a long time, her nose can grow so accustomed to it she can no longer smell it, according to Carolyn. So what does she do? She keeps reapplying it throughout the day. Of course, for the rest of the people around her, that first application was plenty. This, by the way, is an excellent reason to have a wardrobe of scents. Your nose is less likely to tire and lead you to make a mistake if you're giving it new things to smell.

Two Wrongs Don't Make a Smell Right

Many women buy perfumes without properly testing them first. They fall for a scent within the first few minutes instead of waiting to see how the scent wears on their skin. Carolyn says perfume makers know this and design the top notes—that first blast—to hook you. "Problem is, that first rush you love so much fades within minutes. If you don't love the way the rest of the scent—its heart and base—smells on you, you keep reapplying, looking for that top-note rush. Caution! All that reapplying leads to scent overload and torture for those around you."

Your perfume is part of your story; it speaks for you. So take the time to get the message right. Carolyn advises giving scents at least two hours to develop on your skin. "Even better—sleep on it. You'll know the next morning whether it's love it or leave it time," she says. Never buy a scent because you like the way it smells on your friend. "Always test it on your own skin. You are the special ingredient that makes a perfume magical or miserable."

Finally, some women just don't realize how much perfume they have on. It's an innocent mistake, but it's not likely to turn on a guy. "If she wears too much perfume, it makes me think either she doesn't use it very often and doesn't know how to apply it, or she always uses too much and is totally unaware of it. That's not someone I want to be spending time with," says Will, a bachelor.

Leave 'Em Wantin' More

Getting perfume just right is a careful balance. The French call the scent trail, or the wake you leave behind you, *silage* (pronounced *see-yahzh'*). Carolyn calls it "that delicious glimmer of scent you catch when someone walks by or moves in and out of your personal space. It's there and then it's gone, like fireworks or a comet's tail." If you're pumping out waves of perfume and people can smell your scent from several feet away, it's time to turn down the volume. "Use your perfume to lure and tease

and promise, not as an air freshener. You want the guys lean-
ing in closer to get a good whiff," Carolyn says. So how do you
make that happen?

- Start with clean, exfoliated skin; clean hair; and clean clothes.

- Smooth on lotion or cream that doesn't compete with your perfume. (If you're wearing your perfume in lotion form and it has
  a naturally strong scent trail, you can stop with just the lotion,
  especially for daytime. Moisturizing your skin also helps your
  scent stay longer.)

- Beware strong-potioned fruity and flowery lotions and body
  gels plus your perfume. Strongly scented hand lotions at work
  or in the dating trenches can be deadly, especially if combined
  with your perfume.

- No more than four: Unless your skin is really dry and doesn't
  hold scent, you shouldn't need to apply scent to more than four
  spots on your body. Carolyn explains, "I like to spray where my
  body gets the warmest—between my shoulder blades, my chest,
  my abdomen, at the nape of my neck, inside my elbows, and yes,
  between my thighs. Wrists are optional." As a scent warms on
  the body, it drifts up and out, so spray a little lower down on your
  body as well as at your nape. "When you walk by a man who's
  seated, this will give him a better chance of catching your scent."

- No need to rub your wrists together; you risk missing the top
  notes.

- Consider spraying some of your perfume in a small glass vial,
  and dab instead of spray. (You may also want to consider soaking a cotton ball with your perfume and tucking it into your
  bra. The scent will warm and waft up to your nose so you can
  enjoy it.)

• Don't wait until the very last minute to apply your scent. That initial blast, which can be so startling to others, takes at least fifteen minutes to settle down, so give it some time before you take your perfume out in public.

He Can't Tell, But He Can Smell How Much He Misses You

You've now applied the perfect amount in the perfect places and picked the flirtiest fragrance. Your scent molecules are going to that part of the brain that's tied to his emotions, memory, sex drive, and intuition. "If you do it right, he's going to remember it forever," says bachelor Bill. What more could you want? Carolyn says there is one more thing: "If he turns out to be a total jerk and you have to dump him, you have the added satisfaction of knowing that every time he smells that scent of yours, you will be forever in his memory. He may throw away the picture but the scent stays forever." So whether you are sleeping on a bed of roses or smelling the world through rose-colored atomizers, now you'll never let the bloom fall from the rose—or his nose.

ten

Tattoos and Fingernails

Tramp Stamps and Stripper Nails

After years of being serenely single, Gerald was finally ready to find someone he wanted to spend his life with. He met Amy on a popular Internet dating site. Gerald's profile read that he was looking for someone with a four-year college education who was smart, funny, and athletic; who didn't smoke; and who was tattoo free. Amy's profile matched perfectly. After a few short emails and a gander at each other's profile pictures, Amy and Gerald decided on a dinner date. When the two met, there was an initial attraction. Amy was indeed athletic-looking, had a four-year college education, was funny, and didn't smoke. "She dressed a little slutty and had long white-tipped nails that looked a little trashy, but most everything else was matching up perfectly. It made me think, 'Could she be *the one*?'"

When Gerald was saying good night to Amy, that question was quickly answered...er, revealed. Amy dropped her keys, and as she leaned over to get them, her lower back was exposed. Gerald caught a quick glimpse of a wing and a prayer. It was

Amy's tattoo—an angel's wing with a prayer written inside that spanned the length of her lower back. That, combined with the nails, was the straw that broke the camel's back. The wing waved good-bye. Amy didn't have a prayer.

A Doc Diagnosis on Tramp Stamps

Whether it is a lower-back tattoo, like the one that Amy brandished; or one in any other place where women make their mark, the writing is indelible: Men don't like tattoos, even if you think they are sexy or put them in sexy places.

Speaking of sexy places, when it comes to tattoos and men, an unlikely source from which to seek an opinion would be a medical doctor. But sure enough that's where this tale begins. As a resident, Dr. Labib Ghulmiyyah had seen a lot of strange things. However, little did he realize that as an ob-gyn he would see even more. He explains: "I have seen tattoos right above the vagina with men's names or initials printed; one with a fill-in-the-blank that said 'Property of _____'; and a few with slogans such as 'Lucky You,' 'Go for it!' and the Nike swoosh with its trademark 'Just Do It!' slogan next to it."

From right above the vajayjay to sweeping the lower back, it doesn't matter how you spell it (or color it), men don't want their women to have massive or majorly suggestive tattoos. They feel it says something too loud and forward about a woman they don't want to hear. However, not all tattoos (and their messages) are created equal. If you have to have an indelible tag on your body—or already have one—there are some hard and fast rules you should commit to memory when it comes to something as unforgettable (and unforgivable) as indelible ink.

A Stra-tat-gy

Tattoo expert Diane Farris has been in the tattoo business for more than two decades and says that as a general rule, when it comes to getting tattoos, men usually prefer getting them than seeing them on women. However, as Diane explains, "If strategically placed, a tattoo can intrigue and incite questions." She recommends getting a tattoo in a place where only part of it shows. "Leave them wanting more." She says not to get tattoos on "public skin"—that is, skin that is visible in everyday clothes. "Get a tattoo that is only usually seen in something like a bikini. You want it to be discreet, suggestive, and oh so mysterious.

"A tattoo shouldn't be a mark on your body; it should be a means to enhance certain features on your body." For example, instead of having a butterfly perched on your shoulder, Diane recommends having a butterfly with both wings on one side, about to take flight to another part of your body. She believes tattoos should never be blunt, direct, or crass (like the ones witnessed by Dr. Ghulmiyyah and his colleagues). Instead, they should always be left up to interpretation and insinuation. However, Diane underscores that you should make sure you are getting the tattoo for yourself, not for anyone else. "Tattoos are supposed to be a form of individuality and a stamp of uniqueness, not a heat-of-the-moment decision that is permanently engraved on your mind and body."

The Faces Change but Tat Name Remains the Same

According to Diane, the biggest body-art blunder is getting someone else's name or initials indelibly etched into your skin. When considering a tattoo, Diane advises you to think about how you will feel in ten years about what you've decided on and, more important, how it will look in ten years. If you see babies in your future, avoid tattoos in the hip area, as they'll be subject to stretch marks.

In addition, Diane says, "You don't want to come off as trashy with too many tats, and you don't want to wear your thoughts on your sleeve or your skin for that matter." When it comes to too much information, a good thing to remember is that an invitation should be mailed, not written on your body. When it comes right down to it, remember this: Both a diamond and a tattoo are forever. But if you want one (the diamond), you may have to rethink the other.

Another Body Blunder: Stripper Nails

Now that you've tempered that tat and have dreamed up that dazzling diamond, take a look at your hands and move a little north to your nails. Are your hands saying more to a man than you mean? You may recall from the start of the chapter Gerald commenting on the way his tattoo-laden lady, Amy, dressed *and* something else... her nails. He said, "She dressed a little slutty and had long white-tipped nails that looked a little trashy..." Turns out Amy fancied French manicures. She even donned the white stripe from hands to toes with her perfectly pedicured white-lined feet. What looked good to Amy looked trashy to Gerald—and apparently to a lot of other men.

To find out just what men think looks good when it comes to a woman's fingernails and what looks trashy, four pictures of a woman's manicured hand were taken out into the field to get real feedback. The pictures included hands with nails that were painted red, painted a lighter color and extra long (and fake), French manicured (with white tips), and unpainted and natural. When fifty men were asked which fingernail style looked most slutty, like a stripper's nails, forty-three fingered the French-manicured fingers. Are their associations accurate?

From the Fingernail Field Straight to the Strip Club

Enlisted for nailing this due diligence was Melissa, an employee of the Men's Club, a popular strip club in Houston, Texas. After a few days of taking an unofficial poll on how the club's dancers kept their nails when at work, Melissa reported back that out of the twenty dancers she observed daily, fifteen had fake nails while only five kept it real with their natural nails. But when it came to polish, Melissa observed some startling stats. More than half of the dancers had the white-tipped French-manicure-style nails, while only three out of the twenty didn't wear any polish at all. Therefore, the association that men make with strippers and French manicures is unscientifically yet undeniably right on the money.

The Real Deal on Fakes and the French

"There really is an industry-based term with the name 'stripper nails,'" explains Roula Nassar, adding that "the term has evolved to mean any nail or acrylic nail that is long and painted light pink with a stark white line across the tip." And if anyone were to know this to be fact, it would be Roula. Counting on her fingers and toes (and those fingers and toes of a small city), Roula Nassar has estimated she's seen approximately 127,950 nails in her lifetime. She is the resident guru and owner of a popular spa solely devoted to those 127,950-plus nails she's encountered.

According to Roula, men do really notice a woman's fingernails and toenails. "Men analyze a woman's appearance from A to Z. Fingernails and toenails are no exception!" But here's a chance to get it right. To nail down the perfect look and man, keep in mind the following:

- Not too short, not too long—grow your nails to a moderate length.

- Trim fingernails and toenails so that they extend to the edge of your finger or toe at a minimum; however, the free edge of your fingernail (the part of the nail that extends beyond the nail bed) should not protrude from the tip of your finger by more than a millimeter.

- Always file your nails into a slightly square-round shape. Perfectly square nails make him think they are fake.

- Keep nicely trimmed cuticles. If you've got hangnails, he's not hanging around long.

- Apply over-the-counter cuticle eliminator, gently push back cuticles with an orangewood stick or cuticle pusher, and apply cuticle oil and lotion daily.

Now that you've got the tools for the perfect man-attracting nail, how about learning a few of the nail-biting don'ts?

- Say no to French manicures. While men appreciate the neutrality and simplicity of the French polish, the majority don't prefer it. The overtly white line across the top of the nail looks forced.

- Achieve a natural and simple look by using light beige or skin-toned peachy pinks or sheer polish with a hint of these colors to cover the entire nail.

- Try not to get into the opalescent or frosty whites and pinks (they look like Wite-Out).

- Say good-bye to acrylics, fillers, or press-on nails. Period.

- Men find glitter jewels, sparkles, and nail art to be trashy, tacky, and cheap. Avoid them.

- It is better to wear no polish than to have any nails or toenails with chipped polish. Men see chips as cheap and trampy.

- Don't go bright, neon red or ridiculously dark. It may be in the magazines, but men won't understand why your nails are black even if Coco Chanel told you to do it.

Gotta Hand It to Ya

With all the knowledge Roula has nailed into minds everywhere, there are plenty of marvelously manicured happy hands and newly fabulous feet! Now that your hands are ready to express themselves, you can let them tell him how fabulous you really are. Of course once perfected, they can also be very helpful in coaxing and caressing him after you tell him about that one crazy night in college when you and your girlfriends all got tattoos. Even if he scoffs at the tattoo, at least the rest of your body's accessories are right on. Bravo!

GO OUT

A Full Plate of Food,
Manners, and Menus

eleven

Food and the Menu

Harry Covert Dumps Philette Mignon

It was the waiter's third time to the table when Tom chided, "You know what they say about the third time, Emily..." Unfortunately, there was nothing charming about it. The couple who sat on the other side of the table had already ordered and were sitting quietly peering across at her. It seemed the entire restaurant was silent, as if everyone were waiting just to hear her order. Emily couldn't decide what she wanted from the menu or even what, exactly, the menu had on it. It looked as if alphabet soup was the special. The words all blended together with accent marks and hyphens flying off the page. It could have been Greek to her, but it wasn't—it was French.

Emily read down the list of entrées in her head: *foe grass (foie gras), p-ate (pâté), po-u-let (poulet), coke-ow-vinn (coq au vin)*, and *Giuliani (julienne)*. Giuliani? The former mayor of New York? Finally, she saw a word she recognized and blurted out to the waiter, "I'll have the steak tarr-tarr, medium-well, with a side of the hairy-co-vert."

"Pardon me?" the waiter said. The couple giggled, Tom was mortified, and Emily was confused. Tom explained to her that steak tartare was only served one way...raw, no cooking instructions needed. Indigestion ensued, and it didn't take Emily's dessert order of "cream brew-lee" (crème brûlée) and a "caff-a-ow late" (café au lait) for Tom to realize that Emily was not the girl for him. It went down in the book of first-date follies as a gaffe of gastronomic proportions.

Saying "Ganache" with Perfect Panache

Men don't find it attractive when a woman doesn't know how to navigate through her own menu. If you want to win him over before dessert and really impress a man, you must "learn the language, ladies," according to the ultimate maven of menus, Diane Gottsman. As a nationally recognized etiquette coach, she caters to the crass and manages the mannerless. Gottsman says the dining experience doesn't start with manners; it starts with your mouth. When women don't feel comfortable with what they want to order, or how to say it, they look weak and self-conscious—two traits men find highly unattractive.

Gottsman says you should start off with a little dining due diligence. "If you are going to a French restaurant, for example, and want to sound smooth, try to find the restaurant and its menu online, or drop by the restaurant at lunch to pick one up." If you get a gander at the menu before the dinner and see words or dishes you don't understand, then you can look them up or ask a well-traveled foodie friend for a translation. In the meantime, having a few common menu mistakes explained and defined will help you master your menu. Plus, added bonuses come to the woman who has her tasting terms and pronunciations down pat: She may even be able to help her man decipher the dining experience. So it's time to take over the menu, with confidence, aplomb, and perfectly pronounced parlance. He will melt like a molten chocolate soufflé when he hears you pronounce "ganache" with panache!

Below is a list of some of the most commonly mispronounced and misunderstood menu items and culinary terms.

Ms. Malaprop's Menu: A Glossary for Avoiding Soup-er Snafus

AL DENTE (*al DENT ay*) Generally refers to pasta that has been cooked to a state that is still firm, not to be confused with raw or still hard to chew.

AMUSE BOUCHE (*ah moos BOOSH*) An appetizer to blunt the appetite of the guest.

ANTIPASTO (*an tee PASto*) "Before the meal" in Italian. Served as an appetizer and can be either hot or cold.

APERITIF (*ah PEAR ah teef*) A cocktail (usually a predinner cocktail, but it can be had at any time).

BELUGA CAVIAR Fish roe (eggs) from the beluga fish. Very expensive and considered a delicacy. Served in a chilled crystal bowl on a bed of ice. Scoop a tiny serving from the bowl and place on a toasted round.

BISQUE (*bisk*) A cream-based soup with various puréed vegetables and meat or fish.

BOUILLABAISSE (*BOOL yah baize*) A soup usually made with several kinds of vegetables and fish.

CALAMARI (*cal a MAR ee*) Squid that is typically served fried in rings as an appetizer or grilled in strips and often placed over pasta for a meal.

CALAMARI FRITTI Calamari that is served fried.

CANAPÉ (CAN uh pae) A chilled or heated appetizer, eaten with the fingers or a fork.

CAPRESE (cah PRAY zay) Mozzarella served with sliced tomatoes, fresh basil, and olive oil.

CARPACCIO (car PA ch'eo) Slices of thin, raw beef seasoned with oil and spices.

CHATEAUBRIAND (sha TOE bree AWN) A thick piece of steak, cut from the center of a beef tenderloin.

COMPOTE (COM pote) Something that is cooked in simple syrup—for example, pear or peach compote.

CONFIT (kon FEE) A meat that has been cooked, salted, and preserved in its own fat.

CONSOMMÉ (kon suh MAY) A clear broth.

COQ AU VIN (coco VAN) French chicken dish served in a wine sauce, usually with mushrooms and garlic.

COQUILLES ST. JACQUES (KOH keel san jhock) Scallops in a white creamy wine sauce with breadcrumbs or cheese on top, put in the oven and grilled golden brown.

COULIS (COO lee) A puréed sauce of fruit or vegetable.

COUSCOUS (COOS coos) Coarsely ground wheat dish that looks like a cross between rice and grits, usually served under a meat dish or as a side dish.

CRÈME ANGLAISE (crem an GLAISE) A rich vanilla custard sauce.

CRÈME BRÛLÉE (crem broo LAY) French for "burned cream." A vanilla-flavored custard topped with a layer of hard caramel on top.

This layer is usually created by burning sugar with a blowtorch. It is sometimes prepared at the table for effect.

CRÊPE (*kray'p*) A thin, small pancake, usually served with something folded into it. Can be sweet or savory.

CROISSANT (*KWA saunt*) French pastry, usually served for breakfast.

CROQUE-MADAME (*CROKE ma dom*) A croque-monsieur with a fried egg on top.

CROQUE-MONSIEUR (*CROKE miss yeur*) Hot ham and cheese sandwich. .

EDAMAME (*eh duh MA may*) Translated it means "beans on branches." A soybean that can be eaten as a healthy snack or as a vegetable.

ENDIVE (*EN dive*) Type of lettuce.

FILET MIGNON (*fill AY mean YAWN*) A small cut of round beef from the loin.

FOIE GRAS (*fwah GRAH*) A liver (enlarged) of a goose, served warm and whole or marinated in cognac. Also served as a chilled pâté.

FROMAGE (*fro MAJ*) The French word for "cheese."

FUNGI (*FOON ghee*) Mushroom.

GANACHE (*ga NASH*) A thick icing made from chocolate and heavy cream.

GRATINEE (*gra ti NAY*) Cooked with a topping of breadcrumbs and cheese.

HARICOTS VERTS (*ar ee co VARE*)—Thin green beans.

HERB OMELET (*ERB OM let*)—Herbs folded into eggs.

HUMMUS (*HUM us*) Middle Eastern dip or spread made of blended chickpeas, sesame tahini, lemon juice, and garlic.

IL DOLCE (*EEL dole chay*) "The dessert" in Italian.

IL PRIMO (*EEL pu'ree mo*) The first course in an Italian restaurant.

IL SECUNDO (*EEL sehgundo*) The second course—which is the main course—in an Italian restaurant.

INSALATA MISTA (*in SALATA meesta*) A simple Italian mixed salad.

LUMP CRAB MEAT Authentic crab as opposed to the imitation found in packages in the supermarket.

MIGNARDISES (*MEEN yar deese*) The check may be presented with these small bites of chocolate, mints, petits fours, or truffles, served with coffee.

OYSTERS ON THE HALF SHELL Raw oysters served on the bottom half of the shell. They are eaten with the fingers, sipped from the side of the shell and seasoned with a choice of horseradish sauce, Tabasco, lemon, or cocktail sauce, depending on personal taste.

OYSTERS ROCKEFELLER Served with a topping of breadcrumbs and seasonings and placed on a rock salt "bed" to keep the oyster and topping from spilling over the shell.

PASTA E FAGIOLI (*pasta FAZH ee ohl ee*) Italian soup with pasta and beans in broth.

PÂTÉ (*pah TAY*) A paste or spread of finely minced meat. May be served on toast, fresh bread, or crackers. May also be sliced if served in a log and eaten with a utensil (fork), without crackers.

PETITS FOURS (*petty FORES*) Tiny cakes, eaten in two bites and decorated with an icing such as fondant.

POLENTA (*po LEN tah*) Boiled cornmeal served under a meat dish or as a side. It has often been called fancy grits.

POLLO (*PO yo*) "Chicken" in Spanish.

POULET (*POOH ley*) "Chicken" in French.

PRIX FIXE (*PREE FIKS*) A multicourse meal, which gives the guest several options per course. The price remains "fixed," regardless of choice.

PROSCIUTTO (*pro SHOO toe*) Italian ham sliced paper-thin, aged, cured, and often served with melon.

QUICHE LORRAINE (*keesh LOR an*) A pastry shell filled with cream, eggs, meat, vegetables, and seasoning. May be served as the main meal or as an appetizer.

REDUCTION Boiling a liquid until thick, which enhances the flavor.

SALMON, FARM RAISED VERSUS WILD (*SAM un*) Farm-raised salmon are actually raised in fish farms or large containers, with the fish packed in tight. They are fed pellets of fish product, and since they have such little space in which to move, they are high in fat. They are not pink like wild salmon, so they are pumped with artificial color. Farm-raised salmon are not as expensive as wild salmon.

SASHIMI (*sa SHEE me*) Japanese delicacy of raw seafood sliced into thin pieces, served without rice.

SHARI (*sha REE*) Sushi rice, made from sticky, short-grain Japanese rice; an ingredient found in all types of sushi.

SIMPLE SYRUP Equal parts water and sugar that are cooked until they reach the boiling point. The mixture continues to boil until a clear syrup is created. Used for mixed drinks and as a base for lemonade and fruit punch.

SWEETBREADS Parts of the stomach, heart, neck, or throat of a young animal, usually a lamb or calf, and considered a delicacy.

TABBOULEH (*tah BOO lee* or *tah BOO luh*) A Lebanese salad made with bulgur wheat and finely chopped scallions, tomatoes, mint, and parsley.

TABLE D'HÔTE (*tah bluh DOTE*) A multicourse meal with options per course, with the price determined by the choice of entrée.

TARTARE, STEAK OR TUNA (*tar TAR*) Raw beef or tuna served in small cubes.

TUNA NISCOISE (*TUna knee SWAHZ*) Type of salad usually served with tuna. The salad also contains green beans, potatoes, olives, and eggs.

VICHYSSOISE (*vih shee SWAHZ*) A creamy soup made from potatoes, leeks, and onions, traditionally served cold.

WASABI (*wa SA bee*) Called "Japanese horseradish" by some, this item is a combination of mustard, cabbage, and horseradish; it is served with sushi and sashimi. In high-end restaurants, it is considered bad form to ask for more wasabi, because the thought is that the chef has prepared the food with the perfect amount of wasabi.

Waiter, I'm Ready to Order

It may take a little while to commit to memory the terms you've just looked over, but if you use them successfully, they may lead to a commitment of a very different sort—one from him! Regardless, you are sure to impress any man with your newly nabbed repertoire of food and fabulousness. The power to woo him will come not only from the words on your tongue but from your newly acquired self-confidence and assuredness.

twelve

How Food Affects You

Gotta Go, Gotta Go, Gotta Go, Right Now!

I think she is one of those 'crazy girls,'" complains Simon, a twenty-seven-year-old photographer. "She had been waiting for her friends all night. But when they finally arrived for dinner, she suddenly said, 'I have to go.' That was it. She left, and her friends stayed." Simon then explains that he thought his date was testing him. "She probably wanted to see if I would hit on her friends when she wasn't around." Simon's other theory was that his date was late to another date, or some ex-boyfriend text-messaged her and she went to meet him. These were all guesses. But had he known his date's real reason for running off, it would have turned off his interest in her anyway.

Running Off Crazy for a Good Reason

It seems when it comes to men, dating, and digestion, you are damned if you do and damned if you don't. If you don't tell them what's going on, they can misread the situation. If you do tell them you're having stomach problems, you risk turning them off. So what can you do when you just have to go...poo?

"Watch what goes in," says Esther Blum. "It has to come out somewhere. That's just the way your body works!" As one of the country's top dieticians, Esther says women need to pay close attention to how their body reacts to different foods. Some foods are known to give anyone who eats them an unsavory aftereffect, while others are more directed and individual. "When you are going on a date or to a public event with a man, you should plan your diet accordingly, just like you would plan your outfit accordingly."

Gone with Your Wind

No man wants a woman who is full of hot air, much less wants to sit anywhere near the hot air. Avoid the following foods that will leave you with a mean case of the winds: beans, tofu, milk, cheese, cream sauces, cabbage, broccoli, Brussels sprouts, prunes, apples, wheat products, fried foods, carbonated drinks, garlic, nuts, and peppers.

Gas can also come from multiple sources. Esther says: "Be mindful of the combinations of foods you're eating. Believe it or not, fruit is easier to digest on an empty stomach than for dessert." Esther explains that protein digests well with vegetables and fats, and carbohydrates digest well with vegetables and fats, but for some of your fartier friends, protein and carbohydrates don't always pair well together. So what's the perfect dinner for a date if you have a sensitive system? "Try having a steak with spinach for dinner, or go ethnic with lentils, rice, and veggies. Skip the chicken with rice and veggies." Your tender tummy just may not be up for the job of breaking down meat, proteins, and starches together.

A Runny Honey

But what takes you from a bloated belly that's slightly smelly to the dreaded *D*, or diarrhea? "It really depends on your innards," says Esther. "If you have a gluten intolerance, foods like barley, rye, oats, wheat, spelt, and kamut will give you the runs faster than you can say 'Pepto-Bismol.'" Concentrated dairy products like milk and ice cream can also send ladies lunging toward the powder room. If you have to have a dose of dairy, Esther says, "Stick with the yogurt and cheese. Because they are lower in lactose, they are usually tolerated better."

But what if you don't know what is making you go? You have to start studying up because "your body tells you exactly what is going on; you just have to learn how to decipher the clues it gives you." According to Esther, by knowing the clues, you can avoid major embarrassments with your man. "Basically your body is giving you a warning. It is telling you, don't go on that date if you see x, y, or z because it won't be pretty."

If you're feeling sick to your stomach, Esther suggests going green. "Green juices have an anti-inflammatory effect, calm an upset stomach, heal wounds and ulcers, and boost immune function," she says. "If you have a hard time digesting roughage, it's great to add in green vegetable juices to your daily diet." If your stomach is feeling a little queasy but you just absolutely have to go on that date or see your man, there is a way you can possibly pull it off. Esther advises using the herb peppermint. Taken either in tea form or by chewing the leaves, peppermint will relax the intestines. "Peppermint is a carminative, which is a substance that removes accumulated gas from the stomach and intestines." But make sure you use the loose tea herbs, as prepackaged tea bags are said to have lost all medicinal benefits.

Going, Going, Going...and Still Going

If peppermint can soothe your stomach, what can help you soothe that feeling of puffy and fluffy that you get when your body is acting like the Hoover Dam and holding on to every drop of water you've ever had to drink? If you've just had a plate full of fajitas and know you will be retaining water before your date, Esther's got some solutions. "The day of your date, drink dandelion tea throughout the day for gentle diuretic benefits. Unsweetened cranberry juice diluted in water also provides diuretic benefits, as does eating asparagus and freshly steamed or sautéed dandelion greens." Of course, everyone knows that asparagus can give you stinky pee, so if you plan on using the facilities at his pad, keep that in mind.

Now It's Time for Sexy Time

Okay, now you've got all your bodily functions running in sync, you don't stink, and you've got a check on your gas—it's time to get revved up for the ride of your life. According to Esther, a gland-boosting, hormone-balancing diet is critical to sexing it up: "For you babes looking to add more sexual sparkle to your performance in the boudoir, get your eat on." Here's the list of foods for frolicking: asparagus, cabbage, cauliflower, broccoli, tomatoes, squash, zucchini, carrots, peas, yams, avocados, mangoes, papayas, citrus fruits, bananas, apples, pears, plums, peaches, and nectarines.

Esther says, "The veggies will give you enough energy-producing nutrients to keep you grinding all night long! Some can cause gas, so do a test run before going all the way." But if you aren't a veggie lover, you can get a little fruity, too. Esther explains, "The fruits are all chock-full of fiber, vitamins, and trace minerals to keep your blood sugar and your mood stable and happy." So what's the best mood food? Esther admits, "This may seem cliché, but chocolate is one of the only proven foods that acts as a true aphrodisiac for some people." Ahhh...so that's why men always give you chocolate on Valentine's Day!

Funky Spunk

So now that you've got yourself all geared up and ready to go, there's maybe one last supper that could make your sex super. The question here is, Seriously, are there really any mood foods that will take care of what the ladies on HBO's *Sex and the City* called "his funky spunk"? Esther says, "Supposedly a vegan diet will yield some sweet-tasting 'goo,' though it's difficult to find that type of information in a medical journal!" Well...that's what experimenting is all about. Bon appétit!

thirteen

Manners and Etiquette

Eliza Doolittle Does Little
for His Libido

It was a sticky situation that stuck in his mind. Zach had invited his still-trying-her-out girlfriend, Shari, to dinner with a large and motley group of his highbrow friends and their accomplished wives. The group was replete with physicians, attorneys, scholars, journalists, bankers, and, well...Shari. Sure, she was pretty and sweet, but mostly she was kind of unrefined. Zach was the tutoring and perfecting Professor Higgins and Shari, his obliging Eliza Doolittle. Despite all of Zach's meticulous manners mentoring, Shari still had a few rough-around-the-edges moments. But the one that stuck with Zach happened that night at dinner with his friends.

Dinner began winding down, and the ladies decided to order dessert. Shari ordered the molten chocolate cake à la mode. The desserts were delivered, wine was poured, and Shari, proud of her close-to-perfect dinner performance, pounced into her chocolate cake, victorious. A few minutes later Shari and Zach shared a bite of her cake, and some much-needed canoodling ensued. But when Shari looked down to share more of her cake, she realized she was sharing with the entire table. Now what sat in front of her was an apple tart à la mode. Meanwhile, her cake was three ladies removed. Suddenly there was a shriek, followed by gasps across the table. One of the women winced, picked up something, and asked incredulously, "Is this someone's chewing gum?"

Indeed, it was. Dredged out of the delectable pool of her molten chocolate cake à la mode came Shari's muddied wad-o-gum. Zach was crestfallen. His pupil had petered out of perfect and into pathetic. Shari tried to explain that she always placed her gum "on the side." She never expected it would grow legs and travel three seats down the table.

It was too late; Shari's gum à la mode would come to land her in the very same "on the side" position. Soon after that dinner, Zach found someone new. Apparently he wanted to have his cake and eat it (without gum), too!

Mismatched Manners

"It's not uncommon that a man will be the one in the relationship with the better manners," says etiquette expert Diane Gottsman. "It may not be uncommon, but it is certainly unacceptable!" Gottsman maintains that in the movie *My Fair Lady*, Audrey Hepburn's character, Eliza Doolittle, is proof that manners can transcend socioeconomic strata as well as supersede any sticky situations. She adds, "Men revere a woman when she has impeccable manners, even if she doesn't necessarily have an impeccable pedigree." Therefore, if you want to go from flower girl to five-star restaurants in a flash, you may need a little manners maintenance of your own. Graceful, good manners give him a reason to walk your way, while bad manners only give him a reason to walk away. Keep in mind the following tips:

- **Know where your bread plate is, and keep track of your glasses.** The bread plate is always on the left. Your water, wine, tea, or tequila is always on the right, above your plate.

- **Never pick up the whole piece of bread and bring it to your mouth.** Instead, keep the bread on the bread plate and break off small pieces to eat one at a time.

- **Know how to give or receive a toast.** To make a toast, remember the three Ss: stand up, speak clearly, and sit down. Don't confuse a toast with an opportunity to make fun of someone else. To receive a toast, stay seated, smile graciously, and do not pick up the glass to drink to yourself.

- **Know what to do with your napkin when you excuse yourself from the table.** Your napkin is placed on your chair when you excuse yourself from the table and is placed back on the table when leaving the table permanently. Watch your host or date's napkin, too. Toward the end of the meal, if they put it on the table and you still want to order coffee and dessert, you may want to rethink. The napkin on the table is generally a signal; the host wants to wrap things up.

- **When you are going to the restroom, excuse yourself from the table.** It is nobody's business that you're about to go do your business. Therefore, when you get up, simply say, "Excuse me," and leave.

- **Never excuse yourself to smoke.** The person in front of you is more important than the cigarette you want to smoke. A real date killer is asking to sit in the smoking section when your date doesn't smoke. If you do find it absolutely necessary to leave the table to smoke, nothing is more offensive than coming back to the table smelling like stale cigs. Go brush your teeth or pop in a power mint.

- **Know what to do if you get something foreign, like bones or gristle, in your mouth.** Gristle or bones are always removed discreetly with your index finger and your thumb, with the opposite hand shielding the display. Place the foreign object, once again discreetly, on your plate—preferably under a lettuce leaf.

- **Don't walk into the restaurant with gum in your mouth.** If you forget, and you are sitting at the table, discreetly take out your gum by using a tissue. Immediately put this tissue in your handbag. If you don't have a tissue handy, empty a pack of sugar, then remove the gum as you would remove gristle or bones (use your index finger and thumb to remove the gum while covering your mouth with your other hand). Roll the gum into your empty sugar packet; remove it from the table directly into your bag.

- **Know the proper way to sneeze at the table.** Sneezing at the table requires you to lean backward into your left shoulder area, covering your mouth with your left hand. A sneeze is unexpected, but blowing your nose is just plain blowing it. Excuse yourself and blow away in the bathroom.

- **No makeup at the table.** No lipstick application, primping, or powdering while at dinner. If you have a propensity to savor your spinach a little too long, and you suspect it is still in your teeth, then you can take out a compact and hold it down toward your lap for a look. If there is something stuck, excuse yourself and remove it in the bathroom. If there is something stuck in someone else's teeth, it is polite to let them know. Never use a toothpick. Except for Fido, no one looks good with a stick hanging out of their mouths.

- **When drinking, try not to leave a waxy film of lipstick on your glass.** You can leave it on your lover but get it off of the glass. Gently blot your lips on a tissue before taking a sip.

Another way to avoid lipstick rings is to slip your tongue out ever so slightly over your bottom lip as you sip. It will prevent your bottom lip (the culprit) from leaving any evidence.

- **When it comes to your utensils, know which one is on your right and which is leftover.** For example, if you don't order a salad or an appetizer, oftentimes the waiter forgets to remove the corresponding utensil (a leftover). Never use your salad fork for your entrée or your steak knife to butter your bread. When in doubt, always eat from the outside in. The outside fork goes with the salad; the fork or spoon at the top of your plate goes with the first course if the salad is the second course.

- **Never replace chopsticks with fork and knife.** While eating Japanese or in restaurants where chopsticks are the only utensil provided for the table, never ask for a fork and knife. It may take some practice, but every woman should learn how to use chopsticks with ease. It is a huge turnoff for men to see you eat meals like sushi with a fork and knife.

- **Never cut all of your meat at once.** The proper way to cut meat is one piece at a time. The same holds true for the rest of your eats. Don't cut long noodles, such as spaghetti, fettuccini, or angel-hair pasta. You may choose to twirl it using a spoon or nothing at all. Either way is appropriate.

- **Never turn your coffee cup upside down at a dinner to signal that you do not want coffee.** Simply tell the waiter, "No, thank you," or, "No coffee, please."

- **No keys, glasses, purses, briefcases, Magic 8-Balls, or other non-dining accoutrements should go on the table.** Also, stay off your cell phone while at the table. If you absolutely have to take a call, or want to make sure the babysitter has access to you, alert your date ahead of time.

• **Make sure you don't put your napkin in your lap or eat until the host has done so or has signaled that you may do so.** As a general rule, the host is the person who has invited you. If your date has invited you to someone's home or to a party for someone, the host is then the one in whose house you are having dinner. In a one-on-one situation, sometimes the napkin rules get blurred. In hopes of seeming polite, the man may wait for the woman to put her napkin in her lap or start eating before he does. The bottom line is, regardless of who places their napkin on their lap first, don't stick a fork in it until you are sure that the host, or the person inviting you, has already started eating.

• **Don't reach across the table.** Rather, you should ask, "Please pass the salt." Always pass counterclockwise and ask for what you need rather than grabbing. When passing the salt, also pass the pepper.

• **Never wear a lobster bib or tuck your napkin into your shirt.** You will look ridiculous. Enough said.

• **If you plan on paying for him, arrive early and handle this task before the dinner, so that you don't threaten his masculinity by showing everyone that you are paying.** Sophisticates make sure the server brings the check directly to him or her. Normally, the person who extends the invitation is responsible not only for paying the bill but also for the tip.

• **Establish your date's hospitality limits.** This is a nice way of saying: *Hola, chica,* don't break his bank on the first go-round. One of the best ways to glean the green is to ask, "What do you like on the menu?"

- **Always say thank you.** Thank your host, as well as the maître d', waiter, coat check person, valet parking attendant, bathroom attendant, and busboy. And here's a tip: T-I-P. Period.

Foods That Cause Fumbles

The following foods could put you in a precarious position, dribble down your chin onto your shirt, or squirt across the table onto your date. If he isn't keen on sitting in the splash zone, then you should avoid these foods at all costs: whole cherry tomatoes, olives (with the pit), spinach, mussels, crab legs, lobster, crawfish, the "whole fish," any kind of wraps with sauces, fajitas, burritos, moo shu pork or chicken, sushi hand rolls, spaghetti, fettuccini, angel-hair pasta, corn on the cob, ribs, fried chicken, food with poppy seeds or peppercorns, ice cream cones, and profiteroles.

A Seal the Deal Meal

Your order is in, your glass is half full, and now you can sit back and enjoy your company, right? Wrong. Gottsman says maintaining your manners doesn't end there. "Ladies, you can still ruin a great meal with a few unsavory conversations," she says. The litany of hang-ups to your hookups includes laughing too much, boasting and bragging, gossiping, complaining about your health, detailing your recent dental work, touting your family tree, asking, "Do these jeans make me look fat?" and talking about your ex-boyfriends. She jokes, "Never discuss ex-lovers until your current man has sealed the deal." So, if the deal isn't sealed, then just sit back, relax, and enjoy the meal.

fourteen

A Wine Lesson

Putting a Cork in Chee*anteh*
and Cha*bliss*

She asked the waiter for a cup of ice," says Tripp. "I didn't think anything of it." Until he saw what she did with it! "I ordered a very nice Pinot. The waiter poured, we drank, talked, and began to break the first-date ice." Little did Tripp know the ice was about to be broken, literally, right in front of him. While he ordered, his date lobbed, plopped, and plunked a series of ice cubes from her cup of ice into her wine. "Six to be exact. Ice cubes in her Pinot?! I should have just saved the money and gotten her Kool-Aid and a sippy cup instead!" Tripp canceled the next date and iced out the iced Pinot drinker for good.

No More Whining About Wine

From Pinot to oh-no, men everywhere tell stories of myriad mispronounced glasses of "chab-liss," "code dee rodee," and "she-raz." Understanding how to order and enjoy wine is an essential tool to mastering the dating and dining experience with your date. Many men think it is sexy and powerful when a woman knows how to look over a menu and order a great bottle to get to know each other over. The perfect bottle of wine can give you both the opportunity to share its taste, feeling, smell, and intimacy. If you are drinking with him but don't share his experience—or even understand it—then he feels like he is drinking alone. Who wants to drink alone?

As a woman, you may already be at an advantage when it comes to understanding wine. Despite the multitude of previously mentioned female grape gaffes, according to wine experts worldwide, the fairer sex is actually far superior when it comes to the skills it takes to pick a good wine. Sarée Mulhern is one of a handful of top female sommeliers worldwide. (A sommelier, pronounced *so-ma-lee-ay*, is a restaurant's resident wine know-it-all. He or she can tell you where the wine is from, what dishes it goes best with, and how the grapes were prepared and stored.) Sarée says, "One of the most important parts to picking a great wine starts in your nose, and it is scientifically proven that women have superior sniffers!" Sarée attributes the female's heightened olfactory senses to a slew of smelly things. "Think about all the things women smell as they go through their day: shampoo, lotion, perfume, air fresheners, detergent, food, and, of course, men." She believes that because women use their sense of smell to make decisions throughout their lives, by the time they are of age to drink wine, their noses have already been trained to distinguish and parse a potpourri of scents. A man will always be impressed if your nose knows what the wine has in it. "So, ladies, if you say you smell black tea in your Merlot, then sing it, sister, because you're right! It's in there!"

Picking, ordering, and enjoying wine is not as intimidating as it seems. If you study just a scintilla of information and direction, you will quickly be on your way to ordering up an über-sexy, super-sophisticated, tall glass of the perfect Pinot (sans ice). Sommelier Sarée says, "Selecting, analyzing, smelling, and drinking a fine wine is like a seductive dance." So, here's a toast to a seductive sipping of all this intoxicating info.

A Tall Order: Ten Steps to Looking Like a Winner with Wine

1. **Ask Questions.** First, determine whether he, you, or the group wants to drink the same wine. If so, decide which type, red or white. If one wants red and the other white, order by the glass. Jerry Lasco, the owner of a franchise of trendy wine bars aptly named the Tasting Room, says, "Anyone at the table can lead this process, but traditional etiquette directs that the ordering process should be offered to either the senior member of the group or the host/individual who is paying; if everyone is paying his or her own way, then it's up for grabs."

2. **Consider Price.** Look over the wine list and suggest a few options. Both Sarée and Jerry say this is a great way to take the temperature of your date's or the group's financial comfort zone. "You can say, 'What do you think about this bottle of Pinot Noir, or this one?' Then you can judge their reaction to the two different prices." But if this fails, Jerry suggests asking the waiter, "We're looking for a big, bold red in a 'modest' price range; what would you suggest?" The term "modest" tips off the sommelier to offer a few choices in different price ranges. "They usually then observe the reaction of your date so that they can sync up with your definition of 'modest.'"

3. **Match the Wine to the Food.** The wine you select can highlight (or mask) the nuances in your food and emphasize how savvy and sophisticated you are in your date's eyes. This is called pairing. Sarée explains: "As a general rule, you'll want

to pair milder wines (often light whites) with milder foods, so as not to overpower the delicate nuances of either the dish or glass with flavors that are too strong. Likewise, bolder foods and wines naturally go together."

4. **Pronounce Correctly and with Confidence.** On the pronunciation front, Sarée says, "It's hard not to cringe when a well-heeled woman calls Cabernet Sauvignon *caber net savig nan*, when it should be *cab er NAY saw vin YON*, or the beautiful bubbles of Champagne, which should technically be pronounced *sham PAN ya*, since the French don't pronounce the *pain*. It is acceptable, however, to call the bubbly by its American adaptation *sham PAIN*, like how your head feels the morning after drinking it." But Sarée says it is *never* acceptable to call champagne *champ aug knee*. Own the verbiage, own the man.

5. **Labels Matter.** When the bottle is brought to the table, the waiter will present you the bottle with the label facing forward. According to Jerry, "This is the easy part. All you need to do here is look at the label to ensure it's the bottle that you ordered."

6. **Give the Cork the Once-Over.** After opening the bottle, the waiter or sommelier will traditionally present the wine's cork for inspection. Both Jerry and Sarée agree that this should be a very informal quick step of the process. If the cork looks like it's rotten, return it. But Jerry says, "That's rare, so the gist here is to just glance at the cork and then dismiss it unless it looks horrific!" If you suspect something smells wrong, ask your date for a second opinion.

7. **Approve the Wine.** The wine will then be poured and presented to you or your date in a glass. The general rule from the pros: "If you pick the wine, you should inspect or approve of the

wine. If he picks the wine and tells the wine steward to pour it for you, then by all means you should inspect and approve the wine."

8. **Give It a Swirl, Girl!** When you get your first glass of wine, give it a smooth swirl. "The reason you swirl the wine in your glass is to release the amazing bouquet of aromas," Sarée remarks. She also says the swirl is the best way to examine the color and check out the "legs," or "tears" (the drippy-looking lines coating and streaking the glass after you swirl). The legs tell you if the wine is light-bodied or full-bodied, as well its alcohol content. If it is full-bodied, it will leave long legs that streak down the inside of your glass like honey. But Sarée warns: "Be wary of over-swirling your wine, and pay attention! If your date is swirling the heck out of his glass, too, then he's either extra nervous or knows about as much about wine as you do!" To swirl like a pro, both Sarée and Jerry suggest practicing at home with water in your wineglass. All it takes is two or three swirls. They advise moving the wine away from you, resting your arm on the table and using the bottom stem of your glass to move the wine around the bowl of the glass.

9. **Time to Be Nosey.** Now it's time to take a sniff. "You do this to take in the 'nose,' or aroma, of the wine," explains Sarée. "Just bring the glass under your nose and take it all in. You will have your taste buds salivating even before your first sip." Close your eyes and be sensual with this process. He will love it because he will imagine you doing that with him.

10. **The Big Gulp.** You've swirled and sniffed, and now, for the grand finale, the sip. "A lot of people think that you take a sip because you need to see if you like the taste of the wine, but they are wrong." According to Jerry, "At this point the wine is yours; if you chose poorly, then it's your bad." Jerry suggests that if you

are not sure of the taste, ask the sommelier to try it. If it is bad, the wine will taste of pungent vinegar or like a pickle. But if the wine smells divine, then, as Jerry says, "Either nod approvingly or say, 'It's good, thank you.' "

Wine Vocabulary

Now that you're getting the process, here's the fun part and the part men love most: sounding like you really know what you are talking about! "Being able to describe certain flavors and scents you are looking for in a wine helps you find the wine you and your senses will enjoy the most," Sarée says. She also admits, "If you can't remember the name of a wine but know what some of the flavors are called, you can instead say something like, 'I'd like a crisp white wine.' " That's brilliant. She suggests knowing a few flavors to help the process.

When you hear the words "sweet" or "dry," think of sugary and syrupy versus the taste that pulls the moisture from your mouth, like when drinking unsweetened cranberry juice. If you hear that a wine is light- or full-bodied, "light" means it is light in color and tastes more watered down "full" means it looks thicker and tastes heavy. The word "fruity" refers to a lighter and sweeter wine, while "earthy" and "woodsy" describe wines that really taste like they have earth in them or smell of the wood barrel they are aged in. Words like "creamy" and "buttery" refer to the same qualities you experience when you taste something made with cream or butter. These wines linger and have that rich feeling of decadence (without all the calories!). The word "crisp" has a feeling of edge and snap to it, while "tart" and "acidic" are more pungent and pack a bigger punch of dry. They may give you that funny tart look, as if you have eaten a few too many Sour Patch Kids. When you hear words like "round" and "robust," think about a coffee that is described with similar terms. Finally, if something is described as "jammy," that means it smacks you in the face with flavor. Bam! Pick a few of these when describing or learning about what you like as the predominant taste flavoring up your favorite wines.

If you can't put your finger on the flavor you love, then how about good old-fashioned memorization? When you try something you like, remember what it was and how to pronounce it. The following is a list of the most common wines (white and red) and their most common pronunciations. Learn the right way to say the wine, as if it were an SAT or final exam and you are trying to get into Harvard. If you nail the name, it is a huge advancement in your man plan. Soon enough, you'll have him and his glass half full of you! Practice the pronunciations on the following two menus:

White Wine Menu

BORDEAUX *boar* DOH

BURGUNDY BUR *gun dee*

CHABLIS *sha* BLEE

CHARDONNAY *shar din* AY

CHENIN BLANC SHE *nen* BLANNK

PINOT GRIS/PINOT GRIGIO PEE *no* GREE *gio*

RIESLING REES *ling*

SANCERRE *son* SAIR

SAUTERNES *saw* TURN

SAUVIGNON BLANC *so veen* YON BLANNK
(*g* is silent)

SEMILLON *sem* ME *yon*

VIOGNIER VEE ON YAY

VOUVRAY *voo* VRAY

Red Wine Menu

BORDEAUX *boar DOH*

BURGUNDY *BUR gun dee*

CABERNET SAUVIGNON, AKA
  CAB *ca ber NAY so veen*
  YON (the *g* is silent)

CHAMPAGNE *sham PAN ya*

CHATEAUNEUF DU PAPE *shatow*
  NOOF do pop

CHIANTI *key ON tee*

GRENACHE *gre NAASH*

MERLOT *mur LOW*

PINOT NOIR *PEE no NO are*

RIOJA *ree OH ha*

SANGIOVESE *sahn jo VAY zay*

SHIRAZ *shi RAAZ*
  (in Australia);
  SYRAH *see RAH*
  (in France)

TEMPRANILLO *temp ra KNEE o*

Twelve Common Wine Mistakes

Pronunciation is key, but Sarée and Jerry have also given up their list of the twelve most common foibles, follies, mistakes, and mishaps when it comes to wine and all its components. Men notice this stuff; it seems they got the lesson and women didn't, so if you want to keep him in your life (at least until you finish the wine), keep this in mind when you're on your date.

1. Hold the glass by the stem, not the bowl.

2. Don't wear too much perfume when drinking wine—it's hard to enjoy the wine when all you can smell is Coco Chanel.

3. Don't insist that all white wine must be ice cold.

4. Don't insist that all red wine must be warm. When the experts say red wine should be room temperature, they mean the

temperature of an air-conditioned room! Conversely, never ask to have the red put on ice...and never, ever put ice in your red.

5. Don't assume that the man should automatically choose the wine. Now that you know your stuff, feel free to take charge and impress him.

6. It's okay to embrace pink wine. Rosé is great—still or sparkling, the drier the better.

7. Don't order white Zinfandel, unless you're drinking out of a Dixie cup at a frat party.

8. Don't butcher the delicate names. If you can't say it, don't order it till you can!

9. It's okay to spit. It's perfectly ladylike, even classy, to spit wine at a wine tasting.

10. Don't order something too expensive when you're not planning to pay.

11. Don't drink too much—remember Goldilocks and go for "just right."

12. Don't spill on your date—practice your swirl at home with water a few times so you don't launch your red wine across the table.

Don't Whine, Be Divine

Go for it. Order up. Be daring. If you can't imagine doing all (or any) of this on a date, then Sarée and Jerry suggest trying it out during a big dinner with your best girlfriends, or getting them to go with you to a few wine-tasting events. Those places are full of people with their noses so far into their wineglasses they won't be able to stick their noses up at you when you swirl your wine right out of your glass and onto them! Whatever way you choose to learn and practice with wine, by mastering these maneuvers, you will be sure to impress all around.

STEP FIVE

STAY IN

Your Open House and Its Décor

fifteen

Home Décor

Make Your Home His Home

She's shabby chic. He's traditional. She's in love with a mammoth vintage-inspired, yellow buffet on which the paint is chipped, peeling, and faded. He's attached to a beer-cap-studded end table, onto which he lovingly nailed each cap to spell out the name of his college fraternity. Her tastes are great; his...less filling.

They've been dating for more than a year, and this week is "move-in-together week" for twenty-five-year-old Sarah and her twenty-eight-year-old boyfriend, John. It's the merging of lives, the purging of furniture. "His beer-cap table has gotta go!" says Sarah, who studied interior design in college and now works as a vivacious and talented young decorator. John admits she's got impeccable style; he just doesn't always understand it. However, when it comes to the couple's soon-to-be-joint décor, John decides to give Sarah the final say. "All I ask is for a couch big enough so that if I get the boot from the bedroom one night, I'll at least have a comfortable place to sleep!" But, it turns out, when he actually started looking at Sarah's stuff, John noticed a slew of things that he would rather not see. Clearly, Sarah was going to need to compromise on a few of her décor choices.

The Challenge: Honing Her Home-ing Skills

When a woman isn't receptive to even some of a man's desires, the relationship dynamics may begin to shift out of her favor. The opposite seems to be true as well. How so? Well, the experts say, when a man feels he is in a place where he is comfortable, when there are things he recognizes and relates to in a woman's home, he feels a closer bond to her without even being cognizant of the shift. However, when she overdoes it with the feminine accents, his impulse is to move out and move on. A man doesn't want to take over a woman's home— just feel at home in it. This doesn't mean you have to change your entire home to accommodate him, but just a few simple steps can make your home his home, too. Or you may choose to take it step-by-step, adding a little touch of this and a dash of that, to whip up the perfect recipe for romance right in your abode. If done right, it can put out the welcome mat for the perfect man. But if it's done wrong, it might close the door on his attention.

Laura Umansky is one of the country's most accomplished and innovative home designers. Laura, who goes by Laura U, says she has experienced the merge and purge of couples' lives and décor many times over. "Men need a space that has purpose, functionality, and comfort. For women, these three needs translate into ugly, ugly, and more ugly." So how does a woman make her home a place he wants to dwell without trading off all of her style for his comfort? Laura U says it's as easy as one, two, three...four. Her four-step plan incorporates design elements to appeal to male functionality as well as female sensibility.

Step 1: Find the right focal point. If you pick something extremely feminine for the focal point, like a piece of artwork or centerpiece for the coffee table, you are screaming to him, "I am woman, hear me roar. This is where I live; you aren't welcome here." Tone down the rhetoric with something that is less loud and fierce in its femininity. If there is pink, add red. If there is light blue or green, add navy or brown to tone down the female colors and make him fit right in.

Step 2: Have purpose. When men look at furniture, fixtures, and even the way things are placed in the room, they look for functionality. For a man, everything should have a purpose. A clock should be for telling time, not décor; a table should be for putting something like a glass or his feet on; a throw pillow should be comfortable for his head. If things don't feel functional, it feels forced to him. Wherever there are three or more tchotchkes (accessories), one should be removed, especially if it has no purpose.

Step 3: Create the perfect dining and drinking space. If it looks like a bar and acts like a bar, it should be a bar. Add some stools to a kitchen overhang, and he will be sure to hang longer. Men are more comfortable eating in a less formal setting, such as a bar. To them, a dining-room table is a symbol of formality . . . in the food and in the relationship.

Step 4: Get hooked up. The forth step is a lot more involved than steps one through three. For this task, Laura U calls in the pro—TJ Morgan, the owner of a successful company specializing in tricking out homes with the latest technology, gadgets, and goodies. After hooking up hundreds of homes, TJ has mastered the mind-set on how females are (and are not) wired. He says one major thing that impresses men is when a woman hangs her television on the wall, adding, "It really isn't that hard to do; most new construction is actually prewired for this. You'll get major points."

The Hottest Hostess Has the Hottest Home

Okay, now that you have things under control, it's time for a quick-tip-review list and some other helpful home hints. When you are out shopping for your home, carry this list in your purse, just in case you can't remember what you need (or don't need) to make "your home his home." Super-chic home designer to the stars Janna Robinson has styled the homes of celebrities such as Nick Lachey, Oliver Stone, and Paris Hilton. Janna has identified the top ten house items that can turn a man off, as well as the top ten that will turn him on. Take notes, ladies!

Ten Items a Man Wants Out of Your House

1. Bedroom photos of parents, family, and kids. They will undermine intimacy. Put them in other areas of the house.

2. Old, ugly, and mismatched dishes, glasses, and silverware. Having nice things shows that you take pride in yourself and your home.

3. Girly bedding. Men don't want to sleep in the Garden of Eden or feel as if they have been thrown up on by Laura Ashley. Keep the feminine florals for a country home if you're lucky enough to have one.

4. Frilly and overly ornate window treatments. Again think function. They may not know they are called window treatments, but they know when they are ugly.

5. Uncomfortable furniture, especially the main room's sofa. Men love comfort, and they expect a woman to find them something that has style and comfort. Antique chairs that are tiny or creaking are uncomfortable, and so are super-sleek straight-back modern styles. Find at least one big comfortable chair that he can spill his Cheetos in and put his stinky feet up on.

6. A menagerie of stuffed animals or dolls. Talk about killing the moment! It takes all intimacy out of the bedroom when you have stuffed animals around.

7. Pictures and special memorabilia of ex-boyfriends. There isn't a man out there who wants to think of his woman with another man, even if it was in the past—especially if the man was richer, taller, and hotter than him.

8. Self-help books. It is great that women like to be enlightened, but unfortunately men are less likely to be engaged to evolve— willingly, anyway—and they certainly don't want to think that you have a lot to work on with your inner self.

9. Futons. They are uncomfortable and take energy to make into a bed. Men want quick and easy. Futons don't provide any back support, so men end up waking up with an aching back. Limit the futon to just the college years.

10. Prescription medication. Men don't want to know that you are depressed, full of anxiety, having feminine problems, or in need of a little help in the dryness area. Put it somewhere he can't accidentally stumble across it.

Ten Items a Man Wants in Your House

1. Cool artwork and photos. Have you ever seen figurines and knickknacks in a man's bachelor pad? It is always framed music and film posters, artwork, and cool photos.

2. A room just for him. Men like solitude, and sometimes they need to revert to their caves and just enjoy their "me time."

3. Shaving mirror in the bathroom. This helpful mirror saves men from having to shave in the sink, plus you won't have to clean up piles of whiskers after.

4. Sleek kitchen. It shows that you take pride in your home. Men like to see heavy-duty stainless-steel appliances, so that the room doesn't feel too dainty.

5. A grill or BBQ. Men get a sense of enjoyment while grilling the meat and vegetables, drinking a beer, or having a great glass of wine while hanging out with their buds.

6. Luxury bath and shower products. Chances are they won't admit that they use them and they certainly won't go and buy them, but they love using our scented shower gels, scrubs, and the like.

7. Double sink. A man needs his own space in the bathroom. If you don't have one, make sure yours is clean and free of all of your junk (face creams, perfumes, etc.) so he feels he owns part of the space, too.

8. Bathroom TV and in-wall speakers. A man's dream. How great that they can hear or watch the early news and stock reports, or listen to their favorite music before they go to work in the morning.

9. In-wall or ceiling speakers throughout the home. Men will be in awe of this; they can listen to music anywhere in the house.

If you can't put them in the wall, search for a set of speakers you can place around the house that work together.

10. Coffeemaker. Men like to make themselves a good cup of java in the morning to give them that extra pick-me-up. It's like having all of the comforts of their home in your home.

I Got Him to Come Over... Now He Won't Leave!

This home transformation is a gradual process. But as the experts have suggested, it is one that will give you unknown superhero-type powers when it comes to making men feel comfortable in your home. Only one little warning: Once you've given him your tricked-out remote, some surround sound, a bar, a drink, a place to put his feet, and something to put his beer on, then the only thing you'll have to worry about is getting him to go back to his own house! Sorry, ladies; it seems if you end up wanting a little alone time or some of your own sexy time, you may need a separate remote for that!

sixteen

The Bedroom

Your Dream Bedroom, His Nightmare

He awakes in the middle of the night. A picture of a vaguely familiar woman sits near his pillow and stares at him admonishingly. He turns to face the other way. The mound of pillows surrounding him looks like Everest, but the temperature feels more like Miami Beach. He sweats. Covered in florals and fuchsia, he is cramped, boiling, and miserable. She is sound asleep.

That is how thirty-year-old Patrick spent his first night sleeping at his former girlfriend's house. "It was an all-nighter for sure, but not in a good way," he recalls. His recollection is as vivid as a nightmare: "I didn't sleep for fear I would wake up as a woman!" Patrick says his fear of feeling a little feminine stemmed from the flora and fauna that covered the comforter he was baking under all night long. "But the fun didn't stop there," he continues. "I later discovered that the vaguely familiar woman staring at me all night next to my pillow was her mother!" For Patrick, "Mom" was all it took to kill the kinky. He adds, "I didn't even want to kiss—just run for the hills. It was so jarring, we broke up, and I started dating another woman. We slept at my house."

Pillow Talk That Says Too Much

When it comes to sharing your bedroom with a man, you may make some fatal mistakes before you even get under the sheets with him. It's time to take a quick assessment of your bedroom. Ask yourself, what is the purpose of x, y, or z items around my room? Why do I like the smell of this or the feel of that? Try to look at your décor through an impartial eye. Could it be too aggressively feminine for him? The last thing you want to do when you've decided to "go there" with him romantically is to give him a big scare with an overwhelmingly frilly and flowery boudoir. Yes, he may stay over in a room like this, but he'll never stay for good. So get ready for a room with a fabulous feeling for the both of you. You will have a bed that will turn any man's head... and leave him spinning in satisfaction if you just follow a few of these bedroom bests.

Picture This

When sharing a bed for the first time, therapist, relationship expert, and author Dr. William July says women often overlook big buzzkills when it comes to the male psyche. The first, he says, is the framed pictures women generally have hanging around their bedrooms. Dr. July weighs in: "The picture of you and your mother or father, albeit cute and endearing, makes a man feel he's being monitored. He wants you to have close ties to your family. He just doesn't want those ties watching his every move... good or bad. The same rule goes for those cute pictures of women with their pets or nieces and nephews.

They have a place, but not on your bedside table." Dr. July says the only picture your man wants near your bed is the one of him watching over you. In addition, Dr. July briefly mentions a serious nonstarter. "All old boyfriend pictures (no matter how good you look in them) should be put away . . . often for good."

Scents and Sensibilities

Neiman Marcus's Charlie Hinojosa, the rumored "number one nose at Neiman's," says a man's olfactory senses are often heightened around the amorous time he enters your bedroom. If you want him there to stay, Charlie recommends lightly dusting your linens and pillows with fragrances incorporating base notes such as vanilla, chocolate, cinnamon, and amber. "The vanilla and cinnamon are warm, inviting, and edible, just like baked goods, while the amber adds a little spice and kick to the mix," he explains.

Other scented candles and diffusers with these types of scents in them will do the trick, too, but Charlie cautions, "Not too many candles—it's a bed, not a bonfire." He also says to steer clear of potpourri around men, adding, "If they are hungry, they may very well eat it accidentally."

The Princess and the Pea-Size Bed

"Why do women all have queen beds?" questions thirty-four-year-old Mark, who seems to have experienced a sleepless night very similar to Patrick's. He continues, "I never sleep well when I am in a woman's bed. First, the bed is usually too small; there are too many pillows and too many blankets—one for everyone in the neighborhood!"

Home-style guru Laura Umansky suggests: "Start counting. When you reach the number four, stop." She says all a woman needs is a set of four pillows (two standard, two king), *one* decorative pillow (if you must), a coverlet, and a duvet, which you leave on the end of the bed. "That's four different items of bedding, no more than four. Keep it simple."

As for patterns and colors, the obvious pink or floral are wake-up calls for men when it comes to sleep. "The only real way you can do floral is by using black and white prints or dark-colored patterns set on the same dark-color backgrounds, almost monochromatic." However, she says men will often feel right at home with polka dots: "It probably reminds them of that sexy yellow polka-dot bikini."

Laura U's rule of four applies to your sheets' thread count, too. "Sheet sets with 400 or a little less thread count are good because the higher the thread count, the hotter the sheet, literally! The higher the thread count the tighter the materials are woven together, allowing the sheet less space to breathe." She also recommends sheets with sateen blends. "Even if they may have a higher thread count, the blend makes the sheet a little cooler." She recommends shopping at linen stores for sheet sets that say things like "Hotel Collection" or "Luxury Line." And if you are counting, linen sets usually come in fours: one flat, one fitted, and two pillowcases.

This Just In: Mr. Sandman Is Single

Now that you have your bedroom covered, curl up under the covers because if you can count to four, it's clear you'll score points with him. And when it comes to numbers, he won't be counting sheep but instead getting sleep.

seventeen

Movie Night

Classic Male Movie Musts
(and Mustn'ts)

Bryan took his date to dinner at his favorite seafood restaurant. Their food was ready, but en route, the waiter accidentally tripped. Plop! The salmon his date had ordered ended up on the ground near her handbag along with the rest of their food. "She looked sooo ticked off," he recalls. "I thought I would lighten up the situation with a little humor. I said, 'That's it! He sleeps with the fishes,' then I laughed. She looked at me like I was crazy."

After the food was cleaned up, he tried to clear up the confusion, "Have you ever seen the movie *The Godfather*?" She replied, "The Gold Father?" He explained the line to her, but a vacant look was his only reply. Bryan says despite the communication gap, there wasn't a very big age gap between the two, maybe four or five years. "If not the quote verbatim," he quips, "she should at least have heard of the movie!"

However, he figured he'd give her another chance. A few favorite movie references later, including one from a classic,

Star Wars, it seemed to Bryan that just like the book describing the differences between the sexes, he was from Mars and she was...well, living under a rock.

May the Force Be with You

"If a woman can't differentiate between Luke Skywalker (the all-American hero) and Han Solo (the play-by-his-own-rules bad boy), chances are she won't last long in a man's life," says Mike Avila, the executive producer of *Reel Talk*, a popular movie-review program featuring longtime film critic Jeffrey Lyons. Both Mike and Jeffrey cite a spate of movies that women don't know a lot about, yet men feel kindred with, including *The Godfather*. "If you want to understand what a guy and his buddies are talking about when they get together, you need to watch *The Godfather*, parts I and II; skip III," advises Mike. "Every man can summon a quote from either *Godfather* film on command. It's in our DNA!" Mike then provides another silver screen slipup: "A lot of women know the name of the movie *Rocky* and that Sylvester Stallone was the lead, but they couldn't tell you much else. This really gets on a guy's nerves."

Knowing even the basic premises of certain male movies will help you understand how men think, why they react in certain ways, and what silver screen heroes they are trying to emulate. As Mike says, "If you don't know the theme song to *Rocky*, then you'll never know why it makes every guy want to go for a run through the city and beat up on slabs of beef. What a loss!" Plus, you will charm the pants off them if you can throw out a quote or two from their favorite movie.

To start your study, it is important to hone in on a comprehensive list of movies that represent a cross section of men and their ideals. *The Godfather*, *Star Wars*, and *Rocky* are a good start, but in hopes of helping you master your man plan, Blockbuster,

the movie rental giant, conducted a nationwide survey specifically for this book. (The survey results were from a February
2008 omnibus survey conducted by e-Rewards on behalf of
Blockbuster Inc.) Valuable data from men all over the country
was sifted through and organized. So, ladies, press Play on the
following films—you are just a few flicks away from stealing
his heart, soul, and best lines!

Movies that men want you to love. The movies he would
watch on any rainy day, anytime, anywhere (hopefully not
with anyone but you!): *The Godfather, Die Hard, The Matrix,
Animal House, The Terminator, Apocalypse Now, Scarface, Rambo,
The Good, the Bad and the Ugly, Kill Bill.*

Chick flicks that men love to hate. Save these for a rainy
day (with your girlfriends only!): *The Divine Secrets of the Ya-Ya
Sisterhood, Beaches, Titanic, Dirty Dancing, Steel Magnolias, Love
Story, The Notebook, The Bridges of Madison County, Pretty in
Pink, Sleepless in Seattle.*

Romantic movies he'll compromise on. These are the
movies that fall halfway between chick flick and "I won't be
considered gay by my friends if they see me" movies: *50 First
Dates, Casablanca, When Harry Met Sally, Wedding Crashers, The
Princess Bride, My Big Fat Greek Wedding, Jerry Maguire, There's
Something About Mary, Bull Durham, The Wedding Singer.*

Male movie idols. These are the characters he's modeled
himself after his entire life. It is the lead role, the romantic
interest, and the hero, all bundled up into one amazing character, according to him. So here's a chance at learning who he
looks up to: Clint Eastwood as Harry Callahan in *Dirty Harry,*
Sean Connery as James Bond in *Dr. No,* Matt Damon as Jason
Bourne in *The Bourne Identity,* George Clooney as Danny Ocean
in *Ocean's Eleven,* Mel Gibson as Martin Riggs in *Lethal Weapon,*
Vince Vaughn as Jeremy Grey in *Wedding Crashers,* Al Pacino as
Michael Corleone in *The Godfather,* Sylvester Stallone as John

Rambo in *Rambo*, Bruce Willis as Butch Coolidge in *Pulp Fiction*, John Belushi as John "Bluto" Blutarsky in *Animal House*.

Biggest movie weenies. If you say you love one of the men on the next list, he may question you and your ability to judge a man by his character, literally: Ben Stiller as Reuben Feffer in *Along Came Polly*, William H. Macy as Jerry Lundegaard in *Fargo*, Gary Cole as Bill Lumbergh in *Office Space*, Stephen Furst as Kent "Flounder" Dorfman in *Animal House*, John Cazale as Fredo Corleone in *The Godfather*, William Atherton as Richard Thornburg in *Die Hard*, Peter Lorre as Joel Cairo in *The Maltese Falcon*.

Movie quotes to impress your man. If you don't know some of the next few classic lines, you could miss out on an opportunity to bond with your man, or you may miss his point altogether! If you can't summon them up all by your lonesome, at least be aware they exist.

"I love the smell of napalm in the morning." (*Apocalypse Now*)

"You have to ask yourself one question: 'Do I feel lucky?' Well, do ya, punk?" (*Dirty Harry*)

"I'll be back." (*The Terminator*)

"Go ahead. Make my day." (*Sudden Impact*)

"Leave the gun. Take the cannoli." (*The Godfather*)

"That's why I love these high school girls, man. I get older; they stay the same age." (*Dazed and Confused*)

"A martini. Shaken, not stirred." (*Goldfinger*)

"Say hello to my leetle friend." (*Scarface*)

"You're so money and you don't even know it." (*Swingers*)

"You talkin' to me?" (*Taxi Driver*)

Now Your First Scene Won't Be His Last Scene

When it comes to knowing your man's favorite movies, male movie stars, and movie quotes, "you have to ask yourself one question: 'Do I feel lucky?'" If you do, then make a toast to *you*! But make sure you order "A martini. Shaken, not stirred," and to "Leave the gun. Take the cannoli." Because now that you've mastered his movies, "You're so money and you don't even know it."

eighteen

Cooking for Him

A Recipe for Love or Disaster?

Mike read this headline aloud to his girlfriend, Brooke: "Badly Prepared Food Drives Many Men to Drink." Brooke, a notoriously bad cook, rolled her eyes. Mike continued making fun of her, saying had she lived a century ago, her cooking not only would have driven men to drinking but could have just plain driven them away for good. In fact, Mike joked that the only way Brooke could drive men *to* her dinner table was if they were driving a big red truck and were coming to put out the fire!

He may have been joking, but he was really trying to tell Brooke that he wanted her to learn how to cook for him. Mike had grown up with a mother and a sister who could cook anything he wanted to eat, anytime he wanted to eat it. He saw food and cooking for someone as a way to show that person you loved him. Brooke saw it as a waste of her time and a total nuisance. Mike says the more he joked with her about how bad her cooking was, the less she wanted to do it or learn how to do it. He thought all this chiding would drive her straight to a local cooking class or maybe private lessons for the two of them. It didn't, and when he bought her a series of cooking lessons for her birthday, all it cooked up was trouble. She couldn't take the heat, so Mike got out of her kitchen...for good.

Caring = Cooking According to Emeril Lagasse

Not all men are like Mike and need a Julia Child in the kitchen, but most say they would love to have a woman who could whip up something for them if they were hungry that was actually edible, not too froufrou and gourmet but just a basic bite to eat. As Mike pointed out, it makes a man feel like a woman cares about him when she cooks for him. It may be an old-fashioned method, but it works. So grab on to your inner Betty Crocker and start stirring things up. When you turn that oven on, you'll be turning him on, too!

One of the country's top chefs, authors, and television stars, Emeril Lagasse, says you don't have to know how to cook every meal for a man to fall for you, "but make sure you have one good meal mastered!" He believes every woman has it in her somewhere to make something great, even if she has never been taught how. "Men don't need you to make it too complicated," Emeril adds. "We are simple, so start simple." He's a big fan of meat for your man. "If it is a choice between a Caesar salad, grilled chicken, or brisket to win him over, cook a brisket." Emeril says you should choose one meal, like the brisket, and master it.

When it comes to mastering the brisket and everything else a man wants in his tummy, chef Molly Fowler, author of *Menus for Entertaining*, knows the perfect recipe. Molly agrees, "Emeril is right. The fastest way to a man's heart is to fill his stomach with brisket. Men everywhere have fond memories when it comes to brisket."

Molly's menu for any woman's entrée to the perfect mate starts with a simple dinner salad and includes a side of green-chili rice to go with the brisket. The icing on the cake is her dessert, a divine and decadent chocolate cake. But for the main course, Molly serves up her famous brisket, a recipe you can easily put together for a meal.

Molly's Man-Brisket
Serves 8 or more

1 whole beef brisket
2 teaspoons Worcestershire powder or sauce
1 tablespoon celery seed
2 teaspoons garlic powder
2 teaspoons onion powder
1 teaspoon salt
1 teaspoon pepper
2 packets Lipton Beefy Onion Soup Mix
8 ounces button mushrooms, sliced
1 large onion, thinly sliced
1½ cups barbecue sauce

Preheat the oven to 300 degrees. Season the brisket with the Worcestershire powder, celery seed, garlic and onion powders, salt, and pepper. Cover the top of the brisket with the onion soup mix, mushrooms, and onion slices. Pour ¾ cup barbecue sauce on top and wrap tightly with foil. Cook for 5 hours. Open and add ¾ cup more barbecue sauce and cook for 1 more hour.

Cooling Things Off

If cooking just isn't your thang, then skip the sweat, and keep your refrigerator well stocked with his favorites. Of course, all hungry men aren't created equal, but after sifting through quite a few male refrigerators and kitchens, the following choice items were found (or wished for in your refrigerator):

- Strawberries and whipped cream (to go with the *9½ Weeks* DVD!)

- Lunch meat (to help him in his quest to make the ultimate "Dagwood")

- Bacon

- Hot sauce

- Sports drinks (so that people will think he works out)

- Ice cream

- Cold pizza or leftover takeout

- A big, juicy steak

- Potatoes

- Beer—lots and lots of it!

A Cleverer June Cleaver

So if you're ready to move the relationship to the next level, open up that fridge of yours and say, "Honey, this Bud's for *you*." All of this refrigerator stocking and cooking may seem very June Cleaver–esque, but if you are serious in following your man plan, these steps to captivate and win him are a must.

A man feels most comfortable with his comfort food and fixings. Just because you have his food doesn't mean you need to skimp on your own—it just means that you know how to make him feel at home and happy in more ways than one. Men need to know you will nurture them; food is the easiest way to show them. So rather than a cleanup of a broken heart, how about getting used to navigating your neighborhood market? The sound of "cleanup on aisle five" is a far easier solution in the plan to win over any man.

STEP SIX

PLUG INTO HIS PARTS

Nailing Car Care and Ms. Fix It

nineteen

Car Confusion

Getting Under His Hood

It was hot. Tia was sweating. Her car felt (and smelled) like a baking tanning bed. She turned the air-conditioning in her SUV all the way down until the little snowflake popped up. It was still hot. Something was wrong. For the past month, she had seen a warning (about something) on her dashboard LED screen. She had been too busy to get someone to look at it. But she was a smart girl; she could figure out this AC problem. Then it came to her: *Aha,* Tia thought, *so that little warning sign must have something to do with my air-conditioning not working.* She passed a service station but was already running late to pick up Tyson, the guy she had been seeing for a few weeks. It would have to wait.

As she waited in his driveway, a message popped up on her dashboard: "Low Coolant Levels." "I knew it!" she said, as Tyson jumped into the passenger seat. "You knew what?" he asked. "I knew that was why my air conditioner wasn't working." To which he asked her, "So, why is your air-conditioning not working?" Tia responded confidently, "My air-conditioning isn't getting cool because I don't have any coolant in my car." Pointing to her dash, she continues, "See, Tyson, the little warning sign says so." To which Tyson busted out laughing. "Are you for real? Woman, your coolant doesn't have anything to do with your air conditioner!"

Before this incident Tyson thought Tia was hot, cool, and smart. Now he realized she was just full of hot air when it came to cars.

"Parts" in Your Car Parlance

"If I had a nickel for every time a woman confused her fluids," said Barbara Terry, "I'd be driving around in a Lamborghini by now." Why? Well, Barbara Terry just happens to be one of the most sought-after auto experts in the industry. She continues, "If women ever figure out how sexy men think it is for them to know about cars, even if it is just a few things, they'd run right out and get a front seat at their local service center, ASAP."

Barbara says men get really frustrated when women don't know their brand names. "Women can tell a Prada from a Prad-o, in a flash. But put a red Lamborghini right next to a red Ferrari and she'll rarely get them right."

Car and case in point, a well-to-do doctor tells of the time he had just purchased his first Porsche. "It was a hot car that picked up hot women. I went to pick up my date (who, by the way, was smokin' hot), and when she got in the car, she said, 'Oh my gosh, my sister has this car; I love Miatas!'" He couldn't shake that, so he shook her off for good. "I didn't go out with her again," he said, adding, "Now, I get so bitter every time I see a Miata, I am tempted to tailgate." If you get a sense that your man's wheels are important to him, do some research ahead of time by looking at pictures and getting to know some favorite guy brand names, like Lamborghini, Ferrari, DeLorean, Porsche, Bentley, Aston Martin, and Maserati.

Keep the Junk in Your Trunk

"The way you maintain your car says a lot about you to men," Barbara comments. Apparently she's right on the money; a group of guys waiting inside the car wash had this to say about a woman's car: "If she drives around in a mess, her house is probably a mess, and usually, she is, too." Another guy pipes up: "Yeah, and when all that is a mess you can bet so is her personal hygiene. No way I'm parkin' my 'car' in a wreck like that!"

Barbara explains why women should rethink their approach to their cars if they really want to impress the opposite sex. "Men think of their cars as their soul mates in life, which is why they are so meticulous when it comes to their car's upkeep. The typical man will take better care of his car than he will his significant other." Barbara suggests, "If you want to keep your man, keep your car clean!"

Most men say it doesn't matter if a woman's car is an expensive or a brand-name car, as long as it is kept well, serviced, and easy to ride. However, despite what they say, different types of cars say certain things to men about who's driving it—you!

- **Truck.** Tough and unselfish. Having a truck can show that you are tough enough to handle something big, but can also take the time to help a friend move some furniture.

- **Sports Car.** Confident with a wild streak. Driving a sports car shows that you are confident enough with yourself to handle people staring at you, but you may have an unpredictable wild side.

- **Foreign Car.** Business minded. The driver of a foreign car is typically very linear-thinking, almost like a business model. You have arrived.

- **Luxury Car.** Sophisticated and conservative. Driving a luxury car states a level of success and sophistication that the driver wants the whole world to see.

- **Economy Car.** Thrifty. The driver of an economy car tends to be a thrifty individual who is most likely self-confident because she basically doesn't care what people think. Of course, she could just be broke, which is okay, too.

- **Green, Eco-Friendly.** Unpretentious and liberal. A driver that can do her share in trying to keep the world healthy has no designs for material ways... but she could also scold and scoff at a man when he buys that Hummer *and* that Caddie!

- **Minivan.** Family and baggage. There is nothing sexy about a minivan, especially if the man thinks you might have a village of extra kids hiding in there somewhere. In this case, it's better to bike it or hike it.

- **Motorcycle.** Risk taker and rebellious. A motorcycle rider wants to impress her guy, but may have some self-confidence, identity-type issues because she needs such a loud statement of authority and rebelliousness.

Love: Bumper to Bumper

According to Barbara, the smart and savvy woman will never be stumped on what to get her car-loving man for a birthday or a holiday. "She will always choose a gadget or aftermarket part for his favorite car." But if you really want to woo and wow him, Barbara says, "the ultimate gift would be to personally change your own car's oil while he watches." If you really want to rev him up, she says, "Do this task while in a pair of Daisy Dukes! That's hot." Barbara identifies five other maintenance tasks that can help you spark-plug your way into his heart—take time to learn how to accomplish each of these: jump-start your car, check your tire pressure, check your fluid levels, clean your battery posts, and change your tires.

Beep! Beep!

Okay, Ms. Mario Andretti, you've learned the best brands of cars, the clutter is gone from your car, and you know what to do to maintain your set of wheels. Looks like you are ready to get going on the highway of love.

twenty

Ms. Fix It

Finding and Nailing a Stud

Ken will never forget his ex-wife's parting remarks. After a few years of marriage, the couple had gotten caught up in renovating their home. One day Ken's wife barked: "Ken, I shouldn't be picking out tiles and grout colors. Instead, I should be picking out shoes, handbags, and fun trips to Bora Bora." But it was the following snarky remark that sealed the deal for Ken. "She snapped, 'And furthermore, Ken, who cares what color grout goes in the kitchen and bathroom? Frankly, I thought grout *was* a color.'" Shortly after said grout remark, the couple landed in court. It was grout that got Ken out.

So when Ken met his new girlfriend, Detrah, in the midst of a billowing white plume of construction dust, he was thrilled to see she was smiling and happy to be handy around the house. The two met while helping a friend fix a fixer-upper. Detrah loved fixing things, and Ken loved helping her. Together they spent hours fixing Detrah's home—and Ken's heart. Ken taught Detrah about grout and solidified a place for her in his heart. It was a sealed deal.

Home Depot-ly Ever After

As witnessed, learning some basic handywoman skills can help you land your man (and your perfect bathroom!). According to Karla Banner, one of Home Depot's top professional handywomen, "There are certain things a man just never wants to take care of. Men like women who are handy because it takes some of the responsibility off of them." Karla deals with droves of men daily, and she says they are always complaining that their wife or girlfriend broke this or can't fix that. Karla says that when a woman is spotted in the store with a list and a look on her face that says, "I can fix it, baby," then suddenly all the men in the store start to follow her around like lemmings.

But Karla also warns: "There are only a few things men actually think are hot when a woman fixes them. I've asked hundreds of men. If a woman knows too much, it makes them feel a little less needed—never a good thing." She winks and rolls her eyes when she admits that if women don't want to scare off men, then they have to leave the big, tough, scary tasks to the big, tough, burly men. She also jokes that women, no matter what they know how to do, should still be willing to say, "Help, Mr. Big Burly Handyman, I need you to rescue me from my leaking pipes and broken AC unit." So if you're ready to nail that stud down and keep him for good, here is a list of six things men think you should know how to tackle in the home-repair department.

1. **Fix a running toilet.** You'll need heavy-duty household scissors and a new flapper. Remove the tank lid. Press down on the cork or rubber flapper (the large round thing that is covering the hole in the tank) to see if the running stops. Turn off the water supply to the toilet. (The turnoff valve is usually behind the tank, near the floor.) Remove the old flapper with the scissors,

and install the new one by popping the holes on the side of the new flapper into the prongs that flank the hole inside the toilet. Flush to test.

2. **Change a doorknob.** You'll need Phillips and flathead screwdrivers. (Latches aren't part of the knobs, so leave them be.) Remove the two exterior screws from one side of the doorknob. Pull the knobs out of the door on each side. Screw the new knob into the same holes from which you unscrewed the old knob. Tighten the screws.

3. **Hang a heavy picture or mirror.** You'll need a hammer, stud finder, and picture hanger, or a Monkey Hook. Determine where you want to hang the picture or mirror. Know approximately how heavy your picture or mirror is so that you use the correct strength hanger. Use your stud finder to see if the spot you picked to hang your picture or mirror has a stud. Use the hammer to install the picture hanger. If no stud can be found, use a Monkey Hook (no tools required), which looks similar to a bent hanger. Insert the side without the hook into the wall with a quick jabbing motion, like a dart. Twist and push until the entire metal wire is in the wall and all you see is the hook (this should take about thirty seconds, and it doesn't require Herculean strength). The Monkey Hook will hang up to fifty pounds.

4. **Change an AC filter.** You'll need a slotted screwdriver and a new filter. Unscrew (or unhook) the return vent cover. Remove the old AC filter and measure it so you can buy the right replacement size. Buy a new filter. Slip it into place and close or screw shut the vent cover.

5. **Unclog a drain.** You'll need gloves and a small hand snake. Put the gloves on and remove the drain stopper. Clear the drain of visible clogging (hair, food, etc.). Turn on the water. Feed the hand snake down the drain (winding at the handle while low-

ering) until you feel resistance (which is the clog). Press the snake into the clog and rotate the snake while simultaneously pulling it up and out. Withdraw and check out what yucky muck was clogging up your drain. Run water to test.

6. **Recover jewelry that's slipped down the drain.** You'll need channel-lock pliers. If the pipe is plastic, unscrew the p-trap, also called the p-drain, by hand. This is the U-shaped pipe under your sink, which then goes down to make a P shape. You will see two places on the left and right to unscrew. If the pipe is metal, use channel-lock pliers on both the right and left sides. Remove the p-trap (that U-looking part) from the rest of the piping. Empty out the p-trap to get the missing item.

Don't Be a Tool; Buy Them Instead

Karla's fix-it list would not be complete without opening up your box of tricks. According to Karla, if you're serious about "tooling" around, you should have a "kick-butt tool box." It seems men will always respect a woman with a well-stocked tool box. Even if you haven't mastered the list of must-fixes, when he's ready to do something in your house, it's a huge way to gain points in his world. Not only are you making him feel smart and useful by asking him for help with something, you are also giving him the tools to make him successful at fixing your problem. He won't even notice that you can't fix something if you have the right tool box: good screwdriver set, pliers, hammer, wrench, level, tape measure (twenty-five feet), contractor's pencils with sharpeners, safety glasses, latex gloves, dust masks, flashlight, cleanup rags, four-foot ladder, staple gun and staples, box of different-size nails and screws, set of picture hangers and wire, Super Glue, touch-up brushes and touch-up paint, duct tape.

A Finished Project

Now you've got the tips, tools, and tricks to fix up your home and possibly your love life. He will fall in love with your dexterity and adeptness around the house, and the fact that he doesn't have to fix everything that falls apart—including your relationship! But before you get started, just remember the previously mentioned story of why Ken left his mean-talking wife for the mean-caulking girlfriend. Ladies, when it comes to men, love, and relationships, without a doubt, no man wants to hear you pout about grout.

PLAY GAMES

A Sporting Chance at Sports and Game Day

twenty-one

Sports Knowledge

Foul Plays That Won't Play Ball

Carlos was introducing Maria to his guy friends. She had full confidence she could charm the pants off all of them. Carlos told the guys that in addition to being hot, Maria was a big sports fan. She had impressed him with her knowledge earlier in the week. They all agreed to meet at their favorite sports bar to grab some grub and catch up on the games.

When Carlos and Maria arrived, his guy friends were engrossed in a heated conversation. The topic: the greatest sporting finish of all time. James was adamant about the Cal/Stanford game. "Come on, you can't beat a close game that ends in an upset because the other team's marching band walks into the end zone to celebrate a little prematurely!" Bobby said, "No way, the best all-time ending was because of Heidi!" At this point Maria interjected, "First, it was Jessica Simpson distracting Dallas quarterback Tony Romo; now what did Heidi Klum do?" The conversation stopped. "Heidi Klum—the supermodel?" Carlos tried to laugh off the incident,

explaining, "Sweetie, the infamous Heidi game had nothing to do with Heidi Klum or Jessica Simpson." Needless to
say her sports knowledge credibility had fumbled. The other
team intercepted and scored. There was no joy in Mudville;
the mighty Heidi had struck Maria right out of the game.
(Later Carlos explained to Maria that the "Heidi game" was a
matchup between the New York Jets and the Oakland Raid-
ers, back in the late '60s. The fame of this game is the result of
a decision by NBC to terminate the broadcast with sixty-five
seconds left to play in the game and instead broadcast a pre-
scheduled airing of *Heidi*, the made-for-TV version of the classic children's story.)

Maria never really recovered her fumble, and Carlos's
friends were offsides with their derision. After that day, every
time Maria came around, they yodeled and called her Heidi.
It got old and stale, and eventually so did Carlos and Maria's
relationship.

Put Me In, Coach: A Sporting Chance at Love

It's clear that men don't think it's important that women
know every great sports moment, athlete, and team, but a basic
repertoire can certainly help them avoid embarrassing moments
like Maria's.

If you think you already have what it takes to hang with the
boys at the sports bar, then this will just be a review. But if you
don't know your first downs from your touchdowns, it is time
to hunker down and build up your offense. This chapter could
be your lifeline to a solid defensive line, not just in football but
in your relationships with men as well. Someone who knows
a lot about a solid D line is ESPN sportscaster Sal Paolantonio.
Sal has been talking sports on television, on radio, or in print

for nearly two decades and has interviewed some of the most influential athletes and coaches in the sporting world.

Sal agrees that a good way to gain some insight into a man's thoughts and reasoning is to enter through the gate at the sports arena. "Even if it is just a small amount of sports knowledge, it will pique his interest in you. But there is a fine line." You can't be a know-it-all, no matter how passionate you are about learning sports terms, rules, and positions. Let him teach you a little.

One tip Sal suggests is to study online the five basic sports—football, baseball, basketball, hockey, and golf—before you try to learn anything overly complicated, or what men call "something that's too inside baseball." Here he'll get you started with the full name of the league, the playoff name and trophy, the most important positions, time on the clock, how to win the game, names you should know, and a classic movie that you can use as CliffsNotes.

Football

Name of league: NFL (National Football League). There are approximately thirty-two teams in the NFL. Those teams are separated into two conferences, the AFC and the NFC (American Football Conference and National Football Conference). There are around sixteen games per team per year and seventeen weeks in a season. The season runs September through January.

Playoff name: The Super Bowl is usually played in late January/early February. The team that wins is awarded the Vince Lombardi Trophy.

Major positions: Offense—quarterback, running back, and wide receivers. Defense—defensive backs and linemen, linebacker.

Length: Four quarters of fifteen minutes each; halftime comes after the second quarter.

How to win: Score more points than the other team by a combination of touchdowns (six points), extra point tries after touchdowns (one or two points), field goals (three points), and safeties (two points).

Important players: Joe Montana, Tom Brady, Jerry Rice, Dick Butkus.

Movie research: *Friday Night Lights*.

Baseball

Name of league: MLB (Major League Baseball). There are around thirty teams that are divided into two leagues: the American League and the National League. Each of those leagues is divided into three divisions (East, Central, and West). The season has approximately 162 games. The season starts with spring training and ends in October.

Playoff name: The top team in each league plays each other in the World Series in October. The winning team is awarded the World Series Trophy.

Major positions: Pitcher, catcher, shortstop (infield), center fielder (outfield).

Length: There are nine innings, with each team getting to bat and field during each inning. After three outs, the teams switch from batting to playing the field. If the score is tied after nine innings, the game goes into extra innings.

How to win: Score more runs than the other team during the nine-inning game.

Important players: Babe Ruth, Jackie Robinson, Lou Gehrig, Barry Bonds, Roger Clemens, Nolan Ryan.

Movie research: *The Natural*.

Basketball

Name of league: NBA (National Basketball Association). The league has approximately thirty teams divided into two conferences (East and West), each of which has fifteen teams. There are eighty-two games per season. The season runs from the fall through June.

Playoff name: The best two teams play in the NBA Finals; the winner is named champion of the NBA and receives the NBA championship trophy, named after former NBA commissioner Larry O'Brien.

Major positions: Center (one per team), forwards (two per team), guards (two per team)

Length: There are four twelve-minute quarters, with a break at the end of the second quarter (halftime). College basketball has two twenty-minute halves.

How to win: Score more points than the other team in the four quarters.

Important players: Michael Jordan, Larry Bird, Magic Johnson, Wilt Chamberlain, Yao Ming, Shaquille O'Neal.

Movie research: *Hoosiers*.

Hockey

Name of league: NHL (National Hockey League). The league has thirty teams divided into two conferences, Eastern and Western. Each conference is divided into three divisions. There are eighty games in a season, and the season runs from October to April/May.

Playoff name: The top teams from each conference square up for the Stanley Cup finals. The winner is named the NHL champion and is awarded the Stanley Cup.

Major positions: Goaltender, forward, defenseman.

Length: NHL hockey is divided into three twenty-minute periods.

How to win: Score more goals than the other team.

Important players: Wayne Gretzky, Bobby Orr, Bobby Hull, Gordie Howe, Mario Lemieux.

Movie research: *Slap Shot*.

Golf

Name of league: PGA/LPGA (Professional Golf Association/Ladies PGA).

Playoff name: The major championships are the four most prestigious tournaments of the year. In chronological order they are the Masters, the U.S. Open, the British Open, and the PGA Championship. One noted award is the distinctive green jacket given to the winner of the Masters.

Major positions: The leaderboard will contain the names of the players that are important and what position they are in.

Length: A round of golf is eighteen holes. A normal round of golf can take anywhere from four to eight hours, depending on the skill level of the players.

How to win: The golfer with the fewest total strokes for completing eighteen holes wins. In a tournament, games are played on four consecutive days, and the winner is the one with the fewest strokes for the four games.

Important players: Tiger Woods, Jack Nicklaus, Arnold Palmer, Phil Mickelson.

Movie research: *Caddyshack*.

Game Over

You've done it! You've read and studied up enough on your sports terminology to pull off a small (but meaningful) upset in his manly man world o' sports. You may not be ready for the big leagues just yet, missy, but you certainly have the skills to keep him guessing. Don't balk; keep playing the game, solidly and steadily. Building up your sports knowledge and vocabulary, just a little lingo at a time, can move you a long way toward his field of dreams.

twenty-two

Attending and Watching Sporting Events

Game-Day Gaffes

Serena, the woman Trent had been seeing for a few weeks, had decided to get Trent courtside tickets to the Lakers game for his birthday. During their last date, he had mentioned to her something about always wanting to sit courtside. So Serena asked her boss if she could use his front-row, in-the-action NBA courtside seats. When he said yes, Serena surprised Trent with the tickets. But now she was the surprised one. They were sitting at the game, right on the very edge of the court, but Trent was acting as if he were actually playing in the game. He was sweating, yelling, gesticulating, eye-rolling, carrying on, and swearing like a sailor. Serena was embarrassed; what if the people in the seats next to them knew her boss and told him how obnoxious her date was? She had to do something. So, with just forty seconds left until the half, Serena stood up and told Trent she wanted to leave. When he didn't budge and even moved his head around her so he could see the action on the court, she stormed out of the arena. His team ended up winning. Serena was the only one at a loss, as Trent never talked to her again. It was a shutout, without even a thank-you in the final seconds.

A year later, Serena was flipping through the channels and landed on the Lakers game. She cringed remembering Trent. At that very moment the camera panned the crowded arena, landing high up in the stands on a jersey-clad couple screaming and waving their arms at the referee in tandem. It was Trent and his female clone. Apparently if he couldn't find a woman who appreciated his sporting enthusiasm, even if said woman had access to courtside seats, he would just find one who shared it wholeheartedly while sitting in the nosebleed section. As she looked at the couple carrying on and yelling, she was actually slightly jealous. She was still single.

Don't Hate the Playa or the Game

"If you aren't interested in the sport or game, don't go," says Dave, a huge sports nut with season tickets to every game in town. It is the day before the Super Bowl, and Dave is sitting at a sports bar with a large group of his guy friends who are all more than eager to opine on this topic. The men around the table all agree that when it comes to sports, each wants his woman to be a sport about things. Derrick says, "It is great when the girl you are into buys you tickets to a game you want to go to, but if she really wanted to do something great, she'd give the other ticket to your best friend, and opt for a night with her friends." Unless there is an appreciation or understanding of the sport a woman is watching, most men just want women to let them have their alone time with their buddies.

Dr. William July, a therapist and relationship expert, underscores this statement. "Men need this time; it is instilled in them to crave it. I call it their 'cave' time." Cave time is when men get together to do things they may have done with their fathers or watched their fathers do with his friends. Bottom line—it is a time when men don't want you around. July says there are few exceptions to the cave-time guidelines: "Men have cave time with other men; occasionally they will allow a woman to partake in some of their rituals. But she has to know some of the rules before she'll ever be allowed in."

- No fanny packs. It may be good for tourists at Disneyland but not for Game Day.

- No texting or talking. You are at the game with your man; he doesn't want to know about your friends' shoe shopping.

- No rebel yell. You shouldn't engage in any type of whooping or hollering. "Go, team, go!" will suffice. Men can yell; you can enjoy their yelling.

- No questions during play.

- No needing nourishment. Save your thirst and hunger for a break, halftime, or the end of a quarter.

- No substitutions. Subs are fine for the coaches in the game, but don't try to coach the hotdog stand to put the bun on the side. On the side is out of bounds.

It seems these rules apply not only when attending sporting events with a man but also when watching them with him. "The only mutterings or questions you are allowed to ask are, 'Do you need another beer?' and 'Are the chips getting low?'" Dave says. His group of friends laughs, but they are somewhat serious about this. "The worst thing a woman can do is to try and get our attention in hopes of talking about something during a game. You're not going to win, and we're going to lose in the long run," says Dave's married friend Enrique. Dr. July explains that by interrupting a sports competition, you are now becoming a competitor. It is you versus the game. "More times than not," he says, "you will lose." For women who aren't huge sports fans, Dr. July suggests a few options to show the sports fan in their lives that they care about them and their passion for the game.

- **Let men have their cave time.** If you really aren't interested in the game and are going to be upset by his cursing or carrying on, ask him early in the week when the game is on and then plan a massage, mani-pedi, or lunch with your friends.

- **If you have questions about the game, know the right times to ask them.** This may take a little studying up on the rules and game flow.

- **If you are watching with a group of his friends and have a question, never ask the whole group the question.** Instead, quietly whisper it in his ear.

- **If he is an extremely dedicated sports fan, be careful about commercial breaks.** For many men this is not an opportunity to chat or ask questions. He's a master with his remote. During the commercial he will most likely be looking for another game to check the score or watch until his game comes back on.

- **If he's hungry, bring him something to eat.** Think about how nice it would be if you got thirsty in the middle of your favorite sappy romance movie and he went to get you a Diet Coke. It doesn't mean you are his concubine, just that you want him to be happy.

- **No talking on the phone.** He may want you in the room with him, but he doesn't want you yappin' on the phone with your friends or your mother. And under no circumstances should you hand him the phone to speak to his little nephew who just lost his first tooth. It won't be pretty.

- **Allow for naps.** If he falls asleep while watching sports, this is not an invitation to come into the room and take over the television. He will wake up and go right back to the game. A quick nap is part of the game-watching activity.

- **No matter what his backstory is, never comment on the quarterback's cute backside.** Do you want him commenting on the cheerleader's cute "L.A. face and Oakland booty"?

- **Don't be a know-it-all.** If you happen to be one of those women who does know a lot about sports, don't let everyone know it. Men are always pleasantly surprised when you drop a line or two into the conversation about a play. If you give all your information up early, it is like showing the other team your entire playbook. Play smart, stealthily, and conservatively.

The Big Game: Don't Get Punted

Remember, your goal is not to be a sports know-it-all or a sports know-nothing. There are benefits to giving him his cave time and benefits to spending quality time bonding together over something he loves. You just can't forget that there are certain rules and regulations to the world of sports. If you stay within these boundaries, you are sure to score.

GET ON THE MONEY, HONEY

Markets, Money, and Finances,
Cha-Ching!

twenty-three

Learning Money, Markets, and Men

Bulls, Bears, and Bankers, Oh My!

Four New York City guys are out on the town in Los Angeles. They are far away from their high-powered, high-pressured Wall Street jobs and they are ready to start their high-priced, high-partying night on the town. It's not even an hour into their night before Wayne, Tod, Fred, and RJ meet Marci, Carla, Tiffany, and Tracy—four smoking-hot Orange County girls, "raring to get down on the town." As Tod explains: "I don't think these girls had ever met a wallet they didn't like. When I told one I was an investment banker, she said, 'Oh, like you work in a bank...like a bank teller?'" His friend RJ pipes up, "Yeah, when I told Tiffany we were investment bankers in private equity, she said, 'Oh, you're a private investigator?' No joke!" Wayne explains, "I told Carla about the hedge fund I run. I know it was loud in that bar...but she asked, 'You run hedgehogs?'" He laughs, adding, "Seriously? Who runs hedgehogs?" The dating market crashed that night when one of the girls overheard Tod talking to Wayne about "a term sheet for a convertible bond." Tod says, "The redhead, Marci, interrupted us with this brilliant observation: 'I love convertibles,' she said. 'It is very much like 007, James Bond.' "

The Bond girls' stock had plummeted. RJ says it best: "These girls were hot, but they were so dumb and silly, it was just too annoying." All four of the guys seem bewildered by the absurdity of the previously mentioned dialogue. "I don't get it; women can quote you the exact amount of money they spent last week on that pair of designer shoes, but ask them to quote the exact amount of money Google's stock is selling at, and they look at you like you are speaking in tongues," RJ says. Wayne adds that "women never know about money. They don't know what is happening in the economy, how to save their money, or how to make their money grow. They just know how to spend it." Says Fred, "If I met a woman who knew even a little about the stock market or hedge funds, or even the difference between a bull and bear market, I'd be smitten, but shocked!"

Making "Cents" Makes You "So Money, Honey"

Of course, not all men are investment bankers or in the field of finance. But on the whole, it is rare to meet a man who doesn't have money on the mind.

When a woman can talk comfortably about money around a man, "She's money, honey," according to Manisha Thakor, author and one of the leading voices for women when it comes to financial knowledge. She addresses these issues in her book, *On My Own Two Feet*, which aims to help women achieve financial independence. "Prince Charming is not your retirement plan. He knows when you don't know about your own money, and he doesn't think it is cute or funny," says Manisha. After years of speaking with throngs of men about this issue, Manisha has come up with some buzzwords to help women understand the basics. It is knowledge that makes "cents," not only for your dating futures but also for your financial futures.

The ABCs on Do-Re-Mis

Bull Economy. Slang for a strong economy. (For instance, one in which jobs are plentiful, people are getting nice raises, inflation is contained, and there is plenty of growth to go around.)

Bear Economy. Slang for a weak economy. (For instance, an economy with high unemployment, high inflation, and slow growth.)

Net Worth. A fancy way of saying what you *own* minus what you *owe*. May be calculated for an individual or a corporation.

Hedge Fund. An unregulated investment vehicle for sophisticated investors. You can make—and lose—a lot of money in them. They can buy shares in companies outright ("going long") or sell shares of companies they don't own yet ("going short") in hopes that they will be able to buy those companies for less than they've sold them for before they have to give you the shares.

Private Equity. A private bank for companies that need money but aren't ready (or don't want) to "go public." The money typically comes from very wealthy individuals, endowments, foundations, or corporations. The returns can be very big.

Investment Banker. An individual who helps buy and sell companies and makes a lot of money doing it.

ROI. Return on investment; a fancy way of saying how much bang for the buck you got on an investment.

Stock. A piece of ownership in an underlying business. Stocks trade on stock markets, and you have to pay a commission (fee) each time you buy or sell them.

Equity. A longer word for stock.

Bond. A loan to either the government (federal, state, or city) or a corporation for a specified period of time.

GDP. Gross domestic product; the sum of all the goods and services that our nation creates.

Recession. What happens when there are at least two consecutive quarters of negative GDP growth. In other words, it means the economy is shrinking.

Dow Jones Industrial Average. The most common way of tracking the stock market. A collection of thirty companies that broadly represent the economy as a whole.

Mutual Funds. Baskets of stocks and/or bonds that enable you to efficiently put your money to work without having to research each individual "egg."

Federal Reserve. Group of very powerful men and women who set the nation's monetary policy. When they decide to raise or lower interest rates, markets move.

Roth IRA. The classic black dress of retirement savings vehicles. You put money in after taxes, but then you never have to pay taxes on that money again.

Advice You Can Bank On

Now that you've got the lingo down, it is time for another lesson—how to borrow money from a guy. Terrance, a single guy from Detroit, says that "if you need money, just ask for it.

No stories, just numbers." Manisha concurs, and she has three tips to help you let him know you need some help. First, say it straight up like this: "Honey, I need $_____ for _____." Second, she says, "If you plan to pay it back, then say: 'I expect to be able to pay you back by _____." Finally, she advises that you keep it short. Don't tell him a long story. Just give him the bottom line. "Women talk about the emotion of money; men just want the number."

Debt: He Can't Afford to Marry You

Being in debt by borrowing money from a man and being in debt by borrowing money from a bank are two very different types of debt. The saying "A woman wants her money where she can see it best, in her closet" is a sure way to send suitors running for credit cover, according to personal finance guru Marilyn Logan. In 2008 Dr. Phil invited her to appear on a series of his programs as a "financial therapist" for singles and couples all over the country who were suffering from fiscal fiascos. Marilyn says a lot of the stats aren't in a female's favor when it comes to dating and debt. "According to *Consumer Reports*, 85 percent of consumer spending comes from the wallets of women, and a great deal of that is purchased on credit."

For women who are looking to find a mate or even a date, it is time to walk out of any shoe fetish and step straight into a 401(k), fast. If what was reported in a 2006 Oppenheimer Fund survey still holds true—that nearly half of American women would buy thirty pairs of shoes before saving $30,000 in retirement assets—then the number of women who will remain alone in fabulous shoes must be skyrocketing. "Men look at those kinds of numbers, and no matter how good-looking you are, they see your fabulous shoes as a fatal flaw, at least for a long-term relationship," adds Marilyn.

Manisha agrees with Marilyn, adding, "Single women now outnumber married women, and two-thirds of women over sixty-five support themselves entirely on Social Security checks. "Women are the ones left holding the bag (and the debt from the bag) at the end of the day...even if that bag is Hermès. If you've got debt, you may have to choose—the man or the bag," says Manisha.

Both Marilyn and Manisha say all this financial confusion, debt, and future heartbreak could be avoided if women were to take a greater interest and responsibility when it comes to knowing more about money and how it works. "The real issue between men and women is that people who are financially literate or responsible seek the same in their relationships. People who respect money won't pick potential partners if they don't show respect for their own money." Marilyn says she knows many men who've stopped seeing a woman because she owns a $2,000 bag and $1,000 boots but lives in a tiny apartment. For men, "It is really about what the debt represents—justified debt or frivolous debt." Apparently, in the eyes and wallets of a man, frivolous debt is never justified.

He's Not Your ATM or Your Retirement Plan

Manisha worked with a slew of guys to make a top-ten list of real-life lessons, facts, and figures that can figure into your dating future:

1. Have your own investments before you ask about his.

2. Use your credit card only for things you can afford to pay for in full when the bill comes.

3. Start your financial education now. Remember: 80 percent of men die married; 80 percent of women die single.

4. Understand the stock market. Stocks are not scary; they are one of the foundations of a good portfolio. Over the long run, stocks have done much better than bonds, real estate, or cash.

5. Learn to live within your means. Approximately 70 percent of Americans live paycheck to paycheck. Many of your girlfriends are probably living beyond their means; men don't want to date one of them.

6. It will not kill you to budget. Men want women to think twice before spending money on stuff you know you don't really need.

7. Learn how to manage your finances. And no, paying the bills is not managing your finances. Managing finances means understanding how much you earn, how much you spend, and how your savings are invested.

8. Invest early. The money you save and invest while you are young is the most valuable because it has the most time to grow.

9. Make your wheels last. New cars lose half their value within two to three years of being driven off the lot, so they are not an investment. You don't need a new one every year. (By the way, this only applies to women; men seem to be immune to this rule!)

10. Be a teacher. Even though men may use big, multisyllabic words around guy buddies when talking about this stuff, it doesn't mean they really understand it, either. If he says something stupid, call him on it. Chances are he may be blowing smoke. (But do it in private, please!)

Say Bye-Bye to Your Inner Independent Ingrid

A final fiscal lesson, according to Manisha: You need to let go of the financial ties that could bind you to independent spinsterhood. In other words, it is wise to have your finances in order, but sometimes you need to loosen the reins and let him take care of things (or at least make it appear that way). He likes this role. He may hem and haw about the prices of things, want you to know what he's talking about when he talks money, and want you to carry some cash every now and then. But ultimately (and historically) he seeks to be the provider. "Their inner hunter feels manly when they can do this," Manisha says. "Let them rescue you every now and then. And if you can't, then at least let them feel like they have."

She also says that if you feel you aren't carrying your fiscal weight in the relationship, just ask him about it. It may just be your sense of pride interfering. He may really enjoy that you trust him enough to let him take care of you, even if it is just for dinner and a movie. If you absolutely feel you have to pay to make things equal, feel out the guy first. This may be an issue bigger than both of your bank accounts. Manisha suggests letting him pay for the first few dates, unless of course you just want to be friends. "If you decide you like him and you are going on a third date, to dinner and a movie, for instance, buy the tickets online ahead of time. So when you arrive, you've taken care of something for the both of you. This is sure to be an unthreatening way to give him a fiscal hug." But, ladies, just make sure you save the kiss in a Roth IRA and wait for your ROI before you say good-bye!

twenty-four

Gold Digging

Go from Gold Digger to Goal Digger

Nathan—single, handsome, easygoing, and ridiculously rich—was out to dinner with a large group of friends. Just as drinks were ordered, he noticed a thin, stunning, and statuesque blond woman a few tables away who noticed him, too. After appetizers, one of the women at Nathan's table saw that the blond woman had gone to the ladies' room and popped up from the table to follow her. While washing her hands, she introduced herself to the blonde, and then said, "All the guys at my table are in love with you and can't stop drooling over you." The blonde blushed and seemed a little uncomfortable, but the woman didn't stop there, adding, "Especially my one guy friend, Nathan. He just sold his company for $500 million, has a house and a penthouse apartment just two miles from each other, and has like five cars, including a Ferrari."

She grabbed the blonde's hand and ushered her over to the table to meet Nathan. Unfortunately, Nathan's sister Brenda had been in the bathroom at the same time. When Brenda emerged from the ladies' room and saw the blonde and Nathan hitting it off, you can guess what happened next. Suffice it to say, whether she was complicit or not, the blond woman had been implicated in the ultimate gold-digging heist. Nathan never even had a chance to hear her side of the story; his sister made sure of that.

Making Bank on His Bank Account

MAG Hag ("MAG" is another word for "metal detector"), Metal Detector, Pocket Protector, Investor, SEC (Sex Exchanged for Coin), IRS, Finance Finder, Sugah Baby, Baby Daddy Seeker, Barracuda, Russian Mercenary, Black Card Baby, Stripper, Jock Sniffer—all are aliases for the infamous Gold Digger, or woman who only dates men with lots of money. The doling out of the money-linked moniker isn't arbitrary, either.

"Men have even developed their own categorizing system for the gold-digging girls," says J. C. Conklin, author of the book *The Dallas Women's Guide to Gold-Digging with Pride.* According to J.C., the gold digger rank and file starts with the "arm candy." These are the women rich guys consider good for a few dates before they just get too annoying or nosey about their "sponsor's" finances. Then there is the next level of women, the arm candy that makes it to live-in status. These ladies have stopped working, if they ever did to begin with, and have moved in. They keep crossing their ringless fingers in hopes of a money-making marriage proposal. The live-in can graduate to the next level by grabbing the golden ring, along with a very involved prenup. They have gotten married to their sugar daddy and are full-fledged prenuptial "sugah babies."

Speaking of babies, there is one group of gold diggers who skip all the steps and go straight for the big one. It may take them nine months, a few varicose veins, and stretch marks, but at month ten, they'll get exactly what they want: alimony.

A Fiscal Filibuster

Nearly every wealthy man interviewed for this book has a story of how some woman finagled, fibbed, and filibustered in order to finance her life via his wallet. "I'm so over these women," says Greg, a highly sought-after man. "You take them to dinner, they wear designer this and designer that, and they order the most expensive thing on the menu but don't even finish it. And at the end of the night all you get is an air kiss good-bye." He once wined and dined a young gold digger who ordered the most expensive bottle of champagne and the surf and turf. When he took her home, he overheard her talking on the phone. "I heard the little mooch tell her roommate that I was a 'girl's-gotta-eat guy.' She had to eat, and I was there to pay." The woman bragged about her decadently free dinner. She told her friend that the next time Greg called she was going to ask him for a little help with her rent by telling him she had a family member in trouble. "If she thinks I'm that dumb, then how did I make all this money?"

For the Love of Men's Money

Men love money. They love making it, spending it, investing it, counting it, flaunting it, driving in it, and even betting it in hopes of making more of it. The only thing they don't seem to like about it is spending it on a woman who is using them for it. Men detest gold diggers so much that, just as in the story of Nathan and the blond woman, even if you aren't one, if you associate yourself with one, you are gold-digger guilty. But if men spend a great portion of their lives striving to make money and in turn flaunt it when they do have it, then why is it such a deal breaker when a woman is attracted to a man because of it? J.C. weighs in: "They do like to be known for their money, but they want to be loved for themselves, flaws and all." If a successful and wealthy man can spot a stock on the rise in a millisecond, then he can spot the woman who's ready to take his stock and cash in on it even faster. Here are some of the clues that show him when a woman is out for his cash and then ready to dash:

1. Her stats. She can recite from memory the financial statistics; 401(k)s; and car make, model, and year of more than a dozen single men within a fifty-mile radius.

2. Her studies. If you find her Googling, researching, and inquiring about the men she's spotted in the society pages, she's doing her due diligence before she tries to buy out the company.

3. Her job. If she is in PR, event planning, marketing, modeling, handbag designing, decorating, selling real estate, or some combination of the aforementioned, she most likely has a five-year plan that includes a rich man and a million-dollar wedding. She has been groomed for gold digging her whole life; her job depends on it.

4. Her funds. She never seems to have her wallet—or money in it. Plus, she always tells you about how she had to pay for this or borrow money from a friend for that.

5. Her expenses. She has no money, but is a member at the most expensive, exclusive gym in town. Her workout gear costs more than her rent.

6. Her Cinderella moment. She is somehow always at the major charity balls or galas in town, dressed to the nines, while her credit card is maxed to the limit.

7. Her expectations. She has irrational expectations about what kinds of gifts you should be getting her and when.

8. Her body. She knows her body is her best weapon in the war against becoming fiscally obsolete. If a woman has less than 12 percent body fat, there's a reason, and it usually isn't genetics.

9. Her observations. She notices the brand of your watch and can tell you if it is a cashin'-in Cartier or a low-lex Rolex.

10. She is a stripper.

If those are the things successful men say women do wrong, then it is time to learn what to do right if you are going to make it with a money man. Alicia Dunams, founder of the Wealthy Girl Summit and author of the aptly titled book *Goal Digger: Lessons Learned from the Rich Men I Dated*, says it isn't always a bad thing to be attracted to a wealthy man; you just need to know how to position your affections. "Rich men look at most women as wanting something from them, whether that is marriage, kids, money, or stature. When you don't need them for that but instead for the skills that got them that, you are in." Alicia admits to being attracted only to wealthy men, not because they are rich but because they exhibit the qualities that make them rich—for example, they are leaders, entrepreneurs, risk takers, confident, and usually extremely optimistic. Here are some tips to help turn any gold-digging situation into a goal-digging one:

- If Mr. $ offers you financial help, ask him to invest the money for you or open up an investing account.

- Always continue to work. Mr. $ never stops working, does he?

- If you have the money, start your own business and ask him for advice and support—but *not* in the form of dough.

- If you have money in a savings account, ask him about the best investment vehicles.

- You may live with Mr. $, but you should still keep your place and rent it out to create cash flow that you can invest.

- Stay educated and engaged in global, political, and business issues.

- Successful people make decisions swiftly and change their minds slowly. Own this for yourself.

- Learn confidence from him.

- Be focused on one thing at a time. Mr. $ doesn't diversify; he focuses.

- Detach yourself from outcomes—outcomes of the relationship or business venture you want to enter. When you feel like you have something to lose, you become fearful and risk adverse results.

Be the Baller-Shot-Caller You Can Be

You've now got the intellectual equity to make your own deal instead of going after his because as every man will tell you, gold digging is a deal breaker. Don't be the problem; learn his solutions. Once you are free from any need, you can truly enjoy all men for who they are. Learning about a wealthy man's energy, optimism, steps to success, keys to investing, and risk taking is worth its weight in gold. So stop digging and enjoy dating. Every man will consider it a priceless trait.

STEP NINE

SLEEP OVER

A Sexy Time with Sex and Romance

twenty-five

Saying No to Sex

Hooked Up to Holding Out

She would sleep with me but she wouldn't *sleep* with me," complained Sam. He had been dating Marla for nearly three months. They had kissed, petted, and spent many a romantic night together. But romance is relative, according to Sam. "We would start kissing passionately, but it would go nowhere after that. And I mean nowhere!" Sam says this wasn't what he had expected from Marla. He explains that he was first attracted to Marla because she was "the epitome of sexy," adding, "She dressed sexy, she walked sexy, and I swear she could flirt like she owned the sexy player's manual." But their sex life? "There was no sex. End of story." As for endings, Marla and Sam's story ended after a late-night kissing and heavy-petting session on Sam's couch.

"We had been on the couch for hours, watching a movie and kissing, when I asked her to come upstairs to my room. When she said okay, I thought . . . this was it. This was the night!" Sam explains how Marla then got into his bed fully dressed, turned the light off, gave him a peck on the cheek, and said good night. "See . . . she would sleep with me but wouldn't sleep with me! I got more action on the couch." It seems Sam and Marla belonged on a very different couch . . . a psychologist's couch!

The relationship had begun to deteriorate far before the couch-to-bed incident. Marla never communicated to Sam that she was a virgin and was waiting for marriage, nor did she explain to him why she would just stop cold turkey and go home in the middle of their amorous time. When Sam tried to get answers out of her, she never had a solid reason. That was reason enough for him to leave.

Waiting Without Wondering

Another relationship started the same way: Courtney had been dating her college sweetheart, Jason, for four years, was engaged by graduation, and was married a year later. "Courtney was up-front with me about her desires and boundaries. I respected that immensely and agreed with her. She never spent the night with me. No matter what time it was, I always took her home." Jason explains that it would have been way easier to just do what all their friends were doing. But it was Courtney's consistency and commitment to following through on what they both believed was right that made him fall for her even more. After their engagement and graduation, they waited to move in together and waited for their wedding night.

Months before their wedding, Jason recalls the cliché chiding. "Friends and even relatives would say, 'Don't you think you should take the car for a test drive before you buy it?'" Despite the comments and concerns, both Courtney and Jason believed it best to wait. Courtney knew what Jason wanted and why, and Jason knew what Courtney wanted and why. Ten years later they're both happy. Jason adds, "The car drives better now than it did then! Plus, it has never gotten us lost or left us stranded."

These similar stories both had promising beginnings with very different endings. Both men went down similar roads when they dated women who wanted to wait on having sex. However, while one man was privy to the path he was being led down, the other walked blindly into oblivion, frustration, and a fractured romance. It is clear that when it comes to men and sex, women need to make their intentions known.

Opposites May Attract, but They Shouldn't

If your moral compass points north while his points south, your relationship may be facing trouble. Instead, when it comes to a man, it is better to map out your limits at the beginning of the journey. If you have a set of values you adhere to in the bedroom, he may completely respect them—and you for having them. But he can't if he doesn't know about them. And he won't if you play coy and sheepish with your sexual intentions.

"How can two walk together unless they agree on the way?" says Victoria Osteen, when asked if men and women with different value systems on sex can survive in a healthy relationship. Victoria and her husband, Joel Osteen, run one of the most successful and flourishing faith-based ministries in the world. The Osteens preach positivity. Here they provide some important tenets and guidelines for when waiting is warranted. Both warn that when it comes to finding love or sharing love, both parties have to share an important commonality—their morality.

To start, Joel says, "Opposites do attract on many levels, such as political views, financial views, and educational views. But when two people are looking to start a solid relationship, their views on values like marriage and sex have to be cohesive and like-minded." Victoria follows up with, "If you don't look for someone with the same beliefs, value systems, or intentions as you have, you will end up going the wrong way on a one-way street. It will be a fast-paced relationship with a sis-boom-bang beginning, but it is sure to be followed up by a fizzed-out ending. And you may be the one who gets hurt."

A Little CSI Work on His Past for Your Future

So how do you find out if that certain someone you may like is truly like-minded and not just telling you what you want to hear? Victoria says this about Joel and her search for his values: "I watched how he treated his family, how he handled his job, how he talked about other people, how he talked about his boss, and his approach to life. I studied him. Did he complain a lot? Was he negative? Did he do the right thing and take the high road? What was his integrity like?" All tests Joel must have passed—the two have been married for more than two decades. "We waited on a lot of things," Joel says, "because we both believed it was the right thing to do. We were like-minded and we let each other know early on what we agreed about."

Joel implores women to "be up front with the man you are interested in and stop putting off what you believe. It isn't fair to him or you." He says you shouldn't force it into the first course on the first dinner date, but be thoughtful about the timing. "If you are waiting until something comes up in the relationship to bring these types of issues up, then you are asking for trouble. Usually by that time it is too late. You have already invested in this person without telling him what you really want and need. To a man, whether he agrees or disagrees with your value system, this seems misleading." He suggests setting guidelines and boundaries after you have spent three or four dates really talking and getting to know one another. "Men like to know what they are getting up front. No surprises."

But when men find out what they are getting (or not getting), don't they usually run the other way? "If you are someone who sees yourself as valuable and carries yourself with confidence, that projects to men that you have a lot of respect for yourself; it is alluring and attractive when women have these traits. Oftentimes men find them even more attractive than other more physical types of traits." Both of the Osteens believe that being up-front with your intentions, in both the physical and the emotional parts of the relationship, is imperative.

According to Joel, if you aren't ready to tell your date your belief system, then you certainly aren't ready to share other types if intimate moments with him. If this is the case, Joel believes you should take yourself off the market for a little while and really work on bettering your relationship with yourself. "If you are a better you, then you'll pick a better partner. You won't have to settle or compromise your beliefs. Instead, you will feel empowered by them." Victoria agrees and adds, "Even when women have come to the point when they're ready to really own their value systems, they are trying to find someone with the same beliefs in all the wrong places."

Values on Location

Apparently when it comes to values, it is about location, location, location. The Osteens both believe that to find like-minded men, you have to know what you like and have in mind as a good time. If you go to bars, you are going to find other people who go to bars. If you don't drink, why surround yourself with people who do? The Osteens say the best way to find someone who may match your morals is through people in your life who know your morals. "We have seen so many couples meet and marry because friends who knew them both introduced them." They believe that in these friendly-introduction cases, there are very few opportunities to miss the mark on morals. "That doesn't mean you may not miss the mark on attraction and chemistry. That is up to the two involved to decipher."

Another way the Osteens say women can meet like-minded men is through Internet dating sites that allow you to list things like religious preferences or political viewpoints. Also, Victoria says, "If you have a passion for a certain cause, join a group or start a group. Chances are, the people you attract or are attracted to will join, and you'll have a lot of like-minded options for dinner dates!" But, she says, "Don't force it. If you think there might be chemistry, and he likes the things you like but doesn't share the same value system as you do when it comes to your intimacy together, it isn't a perfect match." Joel adds, "If the man you are hoping to see more of doesn't see eye to eye with your morals, that is his choice," Joel says. Victoria follows up with, "It is then your choice to find someone who does!"

Two Become One

According to the Osteens, you can still be the "it girl" even if you decide not to do "it." But making sure you are on the same page as your partner is key. Because apparently this is one of the only parts of relationships where opposites may attract...but they should really try hard not to!

twenty-six

Body Image

Rock It Like a Gold-Medal Model

Christopher turned off the TV, looked at Brittney, and said, "Wow, those women are like freaks of nature." Brittney wondered if he held the same standards for the women he was interested in or dated. Christopher noticed her pensiveness, and asked, "Are you upset that we just spent an hour watching a bunch of women who prance around wearing nearly nothing but a thong, lots of sparkly skin cream, and a set of angel wings?" Brittney laughed, attempting to shrug it off, saying, "I read somewhere that they somehow stretch the screen or the lenses to make the girls' legs look longer and thinner and that they airbrush like ten pounds off them nearly everywhere in the catalog." It was Brittney's attempt to dethrone the six-foot flawless glamazons the two had just witnessed in the televised broadcast of the Victoria's Secret fashion show.

That night she said she was tired and had an early morning ahead. Christopher slept alone. Two days later Brittney was over at his house again, where she noticed the infamous

Sports Illustrated swimsuit issue. The cover's supermodel had her come-hither eyes on and virtually nothing else. Christopher noticed, picked up the magazine, and said, "Didn't we see this chick strut her stuff the other night?" "You actually remember her from the Victoria's Secret fashion show?" Brittney was bitter and Christopher could tell. But now he was annoyed, so he added, "Yeah, I do, and I think she may live downtown because I have seen her like five different times. But what's the big deal?"

Brittney folded and explained to Christopher that when they first started dating, one of her friends told her that he only dated tall, thin, and beautiful "freaks of nature"–type women, which she was not. Christopher began to understand. When he met Brittney, one of her most attractive traits was her self-confidence. Their first few dates were phenomenal. But when they began to get more intimate on a sexual level, Brittney would squirm, twist, and do everything humanly possible to cover up. Why did she always want the lights off? Why did she always scamper around after sex shrouded in sheets, towels, shirts, shorts—anything she could find to cover up? It was becoming a big bedroom buzzkill. He thought Brittney was confident, and that was intensely attractive to him. But her consistent insecurity about models was the very thing that secured his decision to dump her.

Mirror, Mirror on the Wall, What's the Sexiest Trait of All?

It's clear that men like women who can strut their stuff in the day and rock their world with it at night. Men are attracted to power. Beauty has power, uniqueness has power, but self-confidence is the most powerful of them all. A woman who walks with an aura of confidence and pride in herself can be a mere 5'3" in height but project as a six-foot supermodel.

You've seen how some women engage an entire room without saying a word. They just have what the French call je ne sais quoi, that certain something that makes everyone want to be with them or near them. It isn't always looks and legs; it is how your legs carry your looks that locks men in. So, if you think you may be a little low on your levels of self-esteem and pride, then it's time to get geared up and gussied up in order to go out and get 'em!

Who better to find out how to be the hottest woman possible than one of the hottest women possible? When it comes to looking and owning the part, supermodel Karolina Kurkova is one of the world's most successful über-hot women. She has more than a dozen magazine covers (including *Sports Illustrated*'s swimsuit edition) to bolster that lofty label of "hottie." Karolina is single and dates all over the world, but she says all men have one thing in common: "They want a woman with a presence, who is self-confident." She has adopted some surefire ways to kick self-doubt to the curb. And you can, too! She says if you have a hot date, a wedding, or another event and you want to impress the guys there by looking *and* feeling good, follow these steps to successful self-confidence.

Karolina's Man Plan Steps to Supermodel Self-Confidence

1. Two weeks prior to the date or event, cut all sugar, processed foods, and flour out of your diet. You will feel so much sexier, and he will notice.

2. Eat raw foods and drink water with fresh lemon. A lot of it. Raw foods can give you the energy to keep that confidence boosted while also boosting his interest in you.

3. Cut out dairy and salt; it makes you bloated. Men don't really notice, but you do, and it makes you self-conscious—a real turnoff for men.

4. If you have to have some type of sweet taste in your mouth, eat fruit or try popping in a lemon Ricola. It has a little sweetness but is still natural and good for you. And if you need to kiss him...your breath will be yummy!

5. Prep your body for feeling beautiful. In this order, take a steam, get a scrub to get rid of dead skin, get a massage with essential oils to get the moisture back in, and put on a little shimmer cream that has some self-tanning in it for that sun-kissed look. He may not know you did any of this, but you will, and it will make you step out with pep and power.

6. Wear *one* super-sexy thing no matter what. Either a lingerie set, a sheer blouse, a low-cut shirt, or whatever highlights your best asset. If you love it and flaunt it (with moderation), he will, too.

7. Find your own kick-arse mood music. If you have some music that makes you feel invincible, blast it from every speaker you have and listen to it morning to night to lift your mood and self-confidence. You will dance all over his world with the lift it can give you and the power zone it can put you in.

8. You should work out for two weeks before, but if you can't, at least work out on the day of the date or event with him. It not only gets rid of extra water weight and bloat but gives you a little tone, too. Most important, though, it gives you a surge of "move out of the way, here I come" attitude that attracts men all over.

The Perfect Ten

Supermodels aren't the only ones who have to own a sense of confidence—gymnasts do, too! Coach Bela Karolyi has produced twenty-eight Olympians, nine Olympic champions, and fifteen world champions. You may not know his stats, but you will probably never forget his gymnasts, especially the Romanian gold medalist Nadia Comaneci, or the slew of American medalists, such as Mary Lou Retton, Kim Zmeskal, Kerri Strug, and Dominique Moceanu. Bela knows bodies, body image, and projecting self-confidence. "You can't win gold medals without it," he says.

"When I train women, I train skills, but mostly I train mentality." Bela explains that when your body is in shape or getting in shape, it is also training your mind to think strongly and confidently. "Women need this not just in the gym but in life." The more women better their bodies through exercise, even if it is just a twenty-minute walk, the more men notice—not their bodies per se, but what their bodies are resonating. "When a woman exercises, she becomes more proud, more self-confident, nicer, better, stronger. She feels like she deserves attention of everyone, even men." Bela underscores that working out or getting your heart rate up is better than any other thing you can do to make yourself more attractive and self-assured. "If you are persistent, you can change all your male/female relations with just a little time and a lot of commitment." Bela says it isn't too late to start, no matter what age you are. "The physical benefits of exercise may not be apparent immediately, but the mental benefits occur almost immediately." He agrees with Karolina when it comes to garnering the confidence you need for a big date: "Always get a good sweat in before. It will calm your nerves and give you a feeling of invincibility." He says you have to start slow. Here are a few of Bela's steps to playin' like the pros do:

- Look at yourself in the mirror and tell yourself that you are getting ready to take the challenge of working out so that you can get physically and mentally fit. Both your physical effort and mental effort have to be ready to roll.

- Make a decision on your goals—that is, what you are hoping to achieve from this new challenge both physically and mentally. Is it a slimmer thigh, a flatter tummy, and a new attitude about your body and a new self-confidence with your new man? Define these parameters and go for it.

- Start with basic exercises. A twenty-minute walk three times a week is one of the most efficient ways to see quick results. *Gradually* move into specific classes or exercise routines. Often, if you start with these, they get old and you end up losing your drive faster than gaining the boost in your confidence, which is a net of zero.

- Realize the new clique. You are now part of a new group of women who have healthy self-esteem, who are taking care of their bodies, and who are telling the world (and men out there) "I love myself." You will have a superior stride and will instantly look better because you are feeling better.

Even Supermodels Are Sized-Up

If you see successful women who carry themselves well and project a sense of pride and accomplishment, look around them and see how many men they are attracting. Confidence is addictive. And for those of you out there who say supermodels have it easy, Karolina says in most cases you are right, but not always. She explains: "If I'm wearing boxers to sleep, guys are like, 'How come you aren't like how I see you in the magazine?' It can be really bad sometimes because they think that's what they should get all the time." It may sound ridiculous that even one of the most stunning women in the world can lose her footing with a man by briefly losing her foundation of moxie. Confidence is key; now go unlock your real potential.

twenty-seven

Sex

Superb Sexy Time

My neighbor called the police," says Donavan, a thirty-two-year-old, bad-boy bachelor as he recalls the night he and a woman he was dating decided to do the deed. Donavan describes their first sexual experience: "I like it when a woman is a little loud and enjoys herself, but this was like having sex with a shrieking hyena. With all the chaos, it is amazing I even heard anything. But someone had been banging on my door. When I opened it, two cops were waiting for some answers." He sighs and adds, "For a second there, I thought I was a goner, but fortunately she reassured them she was a willing participant...a little too willing."

Donavan's scenario is just one of many sexual snafus men complain about. Clearly, men don't want women to carry on during sex as if they were porn stars. If you are too loud too soon in the relationship, then you won't be believable or make him comfortable. But how is a woman to know what a man wants or doesn't want in the bedroom if all she sees in movies or reads about in novels is, in reality, hyperbole?

Overzealous Could Make Him Jealous

Dr. Laura Berman, one of the world's leading sexual health experts, has interviewed, researched, tested, and treated droves of men, women, and couples across the country and has the lowdown before you go down that road. "Yelling or talking dirty, even if you are truly enjoying yourself, is just too much stimuli for a man to handle all at once," she says, "especially the first time you have sex with him."

"Men want to know that you are totally into it, that they are doing a good job, that you are confident, and that you know how to ask for what you want (within reason)," she explains. "If you want, you can moan and say things like, 'Wow, that feels really good,' or, 'Touch me here. I love that.'" Dr. Berman concedes that "you can even be a little loud. But to scream, shriek, or bring up your tendency to want to be tied up will certainly scare him off." Dr. Berman explains that it's all about balance. She also adds, "When it comes to the bedroom, men want to be men, in the more traditional stereotypical sense. They want to be the only one in your bed, at least in their head." This hang-up, Dr. Berman explains, is actually another big turnoff for men in the bedroom. "Don't ever let him think that you've 'been there, done that' when it comes to sex. Just like women, men actually do need to feel that what you are about to do is special in some way."

The Control Conundrum

Dr. Berman says in the beginning, a woman should let the man take control. But when it comes to the question of who should provide the protection, Dr. Berman is unwavering. "This is an area where a woman should totally disregard a man's machismo and bravado or their desire to 'provide the sexual experience.' This isn't about all that at all. This is about your safety," she says. "Of course it will freak him out to see an economy-size box of condoms in your nightstand. Instead, you might want to keep them in your bathroom." She suggests that when the time is right, you should ask your partner if he has any protection. If he doesn't, Dr. Berman encourages you to say something like, "I think I may have some in my bathroom, let me check." This is responsible and still subtle.

As for the rest of the tricks in a woman's bag or her bedside table, Dr. Berman explains that men generally don't mind seeing a vibrator or some personal lubricants in a woman's bedside table because both are used for self-pleasure. But anything that is usually used with a partner should be put somewhere else. "Again, although impractical sometimes, men want to feel like the woman they are having sex with is not having sex with anyone else, that she is choosing only them." Dr. Berman says that just like women, men don't like to feel as if they are only an instrument of your pleasure or that they could be replaced by any ol' Joe. When they see a cadre of toys and lotions, they automatically picture you using them with other men. This image they've conjured up of you with another man kills their libido. This also gets them wondering, "Where am I in her lineup of men who she keeps around solely for pleasing herself?" Dr. Berman recommends that in the beginning of a sexual relationship, a touch of demureness goes a long way with men. "Demureness doesn't equate to being a prude. Just use some discretion at the start of a sexual relationship. Wait a little while, then you can go do your wild thing once you and your partner know each other better."

Now *This* Is Novel

Just because he doesn't want to see you brazenly flaunting your novelties and sex toys doesn't mean you shouldn't have them at all. Dr. Berman explains that novelty items in a relationship are important for keeping things fresh. They can also provide men with fodder for a sexual foreshadowing of sorts. "Men need novelty and newness. They thrive on it. It is in their DNA." She advises, "If it is around the third or fourth time you and your partner are having sex, you should try something slightly different and mildly adventurous." But why? Isn't the fact that you are actually having sex with him adventurous enough? Dr. Berman says doing something different or tying something early on gives him the signal that you are open to that sort of stuff and that you would be someone who would be fun to have a long-term sexual relationship with, including the fact that you are already fun to have sex with in the here and now. "Men search for women who are confident and open to novelty, have enthusiasm for trying new things, and even introduce them into the relationship."

So, if you've reached a point where you feel comfortable with your partner and want to introduce a little surprise into the bedroom, consider the following (in this adventurous order): try a new position; try it in front of a mirror or somewhere other than the bed; try a striptease for him; add fun foods such as whipped cream, honey, chocolate, or Nutella; incorporate some intimacy-enhancing products such as K-Y brand's Yours and Mine couple's lubricant or KamaSutra's Honey Dust (yummy!); charge up the battery-operated toys like the Ladybug or the Dolphin; get into some role-playing.

Novelty Nancy and Her Halloween All Year!

When it comes to role-playing, why wait until the end of October to show him that Dorothy not only lost her dog, Toto, but also lost half of her dress, and that Captain Hook has turned into Captain Hooker? Men love seeing the smutty parade of pixies and pirates on Halloween—and any other day of the week. Whether it's a storybook or superhero character you choose to role-play with, smutting up the fond familiarities of your childhood is actually a big turn-on for men. But why are saucy storybook characters and slutty superheroes such a success?

Another one of the country's top experts in women's sexual health, Dr. Christopher Jayne, explains, "These childhood characters can often remind men of a time when they were younger and free of any real responsibilities or burdens. The role-playing of these storybook characters such as Little Red Riding Hood or Little Bo Peep can make men feel that free youthfulness again." Dr. Jayne says the images conjure up a sense of virility and viability that he may have lost somewhere in all of his responsibilities, jobs, and daily tasks. Dr. Berman agrees, "Making a man feel free and youthful again can turn up his interest and the heat in any stale sexual relationship."

Fakes Are Flakes

Now that you know how to keep it fresh, it's time to learn how and why to keep from faking it. Dr. Berman is a big believer in the "*no* fakes allowed" policy. She says that if he asks you how the sex was for you, there's no need to tell him it was horrible. "But don't give credit where credit is not due, especially if you think you are going to have sex with him in the future." She says when women do this, they begin to set up a cycle of resentment and unrealistic expectations. "He will eventually find out that you lied, because at some point you are going to get sick of faking it and get resentful that you have to for so long." She advises that if, after sex, your man asks, "Did you have an orgasm?" you should be honest and delicate. She suggests you say something like, "No, I didn't. But it usually takes me a while before I do. Regardless, it felt amazing and I was really close." Furthermore, she says, "If they don't ask, then don't ever volunteer that information; that's just adding insult to injury." It seems that, oftentimes, men need your orgasm more than you need it! "But this is no reason not to stay true to you."

Dr. Berman explains that many women can't have an orgasm every time, or they have orgasms that may vary in intensity. "Orgasms are great when they happen, but they aren't essential." According to Dr. Berman's research, the number one predictor of a woman's sexual satisfaction is not whether she reaches orgasm or how many orgasms she's had. Instead, it is the intimacy and the connection she feels with the person she is having sex with.

Feeling connected and comfortable with your partner is an essential part of a woman's sexual experience. But to really take it to the next level with a man, Dr. Berman says you need to really be comfortable with you—everything about you—flaws and all. One thing that can take away from a man's sensory adventure is when you insist on having the lights off—all of them. Yes, men feel you, but they want to see you. That is why, according to Dr. Berman, they get so aroused when women are in the position on top of them. "In this position they can not only see your breasts, but can take visual cues from your face and see that you are just as into it as they are." Dr. Berman adds that men can't stand it when a woman gets up from the bed to go to the bathroom or get some water and she cloaks herself in the entire bed set. "It is really a turn-on to men when a nude woman just pops out of bed and casually walks to the bathroom or kitchen if she wants something." She explains that when a woman does something like that, a man says to himself, "Now here's a girl who I can have fun with and who is comfortable with her body. That's hot!"

Your Period—Their Question Mark on Sex

Okay, now you may be perfectly comfortable with you. That's great! But don't take this comfort level too far. Even comfort has its uncomfortable moments—like that time of the month when Aunt Flo decides to come to town. Dr. Berman suggests that when it comes down to whether you want to introduce your man to your aunt, you may want to give him the option to decline the introduction. In fact, many a man can tell you a story of sleeping with women who either didn't tell them or didn't know they were having their periods. Don't be that girl. From frat houses to bars and clubs everywhere, men swap stories about "that girl." They even have a code name for her—Bloody Mary.

Nicknames aside, Dr. Berman says that women should be vigilant with their cycles, especially if they are sexually active. "It is only fair to let your partner know you are menstruating and let him decide on whether he wants to proceed." She explains that some men have differing opinions when it comes to a woman's period and sex. "It depends on how they were raised and what kind of general messages they received about women. The more empowering, positive, modern, and feminist the message they heard when they were young men, the less likely they are to incorporate gender scripting and be bothered by your period. Conversely, men who grew up not talking about women's issues will generally not want to have anything to do with "it." Period.

An option for women with partners who want to have sex while she is menstruating is to try some of the lesser-known feminine products designed for this occasion. These products look and act like little diaphragms, or "cups," according to Dr. Berman. They are pliable-looking spheres that are inserted vaginally by squeezing both sides of the circle and then gently pushing in and upward. While diaphragms act to keep the egg and sperm separated, these types of products work by keeping your menstrual fluids on one side (your side) while keeping him clean on the other side. Dr. Berman says these products are totally safe and act as good options, but she warns that they do not act as birth control or help prevent STDs.

Don't Do the Math

While STDs are certainly not a sexy topic if you are planning to have sex, they should be discussed. "This isn't a time to get the numbers on your man," admonishes Dr. Berman. "It isn't important how many sexual partners he's had, but it is important if any of those partners had an STD or if your partner has one." When it comes to STDs, Dr. Berman implores women to ask their partners for a brief sexual history. "This isn't a lengthy conversation with details on how, who, or why, just the facts."

In fact, she doesn't recommend talking about your past sexual relationships or any of your relationships at all except from the standpoint of what you've learned or any personal growth you experienced because of it. In general, don't talk about the other men in your past if you want to keep the man you currently have in your life as part of your life for good. According to Dr. Berman, if you boast about your past sexual experiences, you will only lesson his libido and turn him off. "It is not that men expect you to be a virgin, but if you give him even a brief glimpse at what you've been up to or who you've had sexual relations with before him, he gets grossed out. Men hate imagining you with another man, but they are preprogrammed to do so."

Man-ogomy versus Woman-ogomy

So if men can't tolerate the image of you having sex with men other than themselves, then why are they busy trying to have sex with you and multitudes of other women at the same time? Don't they feel your pain? "Nope," says Dr. Berman.

"Since caveman days, men have been programmed to have sex with as many women as possible. Men were supposed to spread their genes as far and wide as they could. You can't change their physical and historical makeup."

According to Dr. Berman, it is natural that men will always want to have sex with a lot of different people, even if intellectually, socially, and emotionally it seems they only want to have sex with you. She advises that if you want to circumvent the rotating-women phenomenon and steer him solely toward the thought of having only one partner, then you need to provide him with a sense of variation. Dr. Berman says that for a man, monogamy is possible, and that if a little imagination and creativity are added to the mix, then sex with the same woman can actually be very different. She recommends women take the lead in this arena. "It keeps him on his toes, wondering what she is going to bring to the boudoir next." Dr. Berman underscores that women need to keep the adventure and newness by providing a slew of different and exciting new things to try with him. It seems that if you try new things in the bedroom, he won't try new women in it, either.

Knowledge Is Power but So Is Knowing You Can Wait

All of this information will be helpful in your quest to perfect your very own man plan. But if it isn't in the plan to have sex with your man because you want to wait, then store it away. There is bound to be a rainy day when you and your man may want to play. But until then, it is at least good to know that you have the power to make the decisions when it comes to jumping in bed or waiting on sex. That is the most powerful and sexy position of them all!

TALK LESS
BUT SAY MORE

The Blah, Blah, Blah
on Conversation and Communication

twenty-eight

Body Language

Let 'Em Hear Your Body Talk

Once, a woman walked up to me, placed her business card in my hand, and said, 'If you know what is good for you, then call me.' She wasn't a lawyer, doctor, masseuse, or call girl. So she clearly didn't know what was good for me." Thirty-eight-year-old Ken has been in more than one situation where the woman has been the aggressor, and each time he has been more turned off than flattered. His friends Christian and Roberto agree that women shouldn't be the ones doing the picking up. Christian jokes, "The only reason a woman should verbally hit on a man is to get ahead in the workplace, to find out if he has the money to pay off her credit cards, or to get a better tip at the end of his lengthy and boring dinner with his wife."

Ken pipes up, "I think most men prefer it when a woman has an air of mystery about her. A woman who uses her body instead of her mouth to let a guy know 'It's cool to come over here' makes the chase a lot more rewarding." Christian tells the group his theory. "If a woman makes a blatant move on me, I am suspicious of her motives." He adds, "Let's say she asks me something as simple as, 'Can I buy you a drink?' Instantly I know something is wrong with her." Christian opines, "Women are way too smart and maneuvering to ever be that straightforward. They would never reveal an ounce of vulnerability without a reason. They always have something else going on behind the scenes."

Get Physical

From aggressively bad pickup lines to the oh-so-simple ones, it's obvious that even though women have broken free of many gender stereotypes, men still want to be the ones to initiate contact. That's their job. When it comes to showing someone you are interested, it seems old-school pickups are the best pickups. So what should a woman's role be in the game?

Jan Hargrave, one of the country's leading experts in nonverbal communication (also known as body language), explains: "A woman's role in this type of coquetry is to send men clues with her body language. These are hints that hit men in their subconscious and then trigger their arousal and intent." Jan adds that just a tilt this way or a shoulder dip that way can trigger their ardor. "Conversely, there are a slew of different signals you can send him to let him know it's a no-go or to divine whether or not his body language is saying he is into you!"

Some Science to Back Up the Body

It's well known in the communications community that nonverbal aspects of communication make up 93 percent of a message, while only 7 percent of the impact is verbal. In fact, the two differ so much that studies indicate that whenever a person's nonverbal communication doesn't match up with his or her verbal communication, the listener will almost always believe the nonverbal communication over the verbal communication. "Your posture, stance, mannerisms, facial movements, legs, feet, and even your curves reveal more about you to a man than your words ever can," says Jan. She believes that developing a comprehensive knowledge of nonverbal courtship gestures can also help you determine the meaning and intention of men. To really own the market on men, it is time to awaken the instinctive knowledge about human nature lying dormant in your subconscious. The following two lists summarize some of the major body language clues you both might display.

Fifteen Body Language Signs That Show His Interest in You

1. He will lean forward.

2. The front of his body will face you directly.

3. He will tilt his head.

4. He will sit on the edge of his chair to get closer to you.

5. He will touch his face often, especially as he looks at you.

6. He will smile either at you or to himself when you are around. This is an unconscious way for him to look appealing and draw attention to himself.

7. He will display grooming behaviors (slick his hair down, straighten his tie, and check his teeth).

8. He will exaggerate body movements to get you to notice him.

9. He will moisten his lips.

10. He will play with his clothes; predominantly, he will pull up his socks.

11. He will touch you briefly, accidentally or on purpose.

12. He will laugh or clear his throat to get your attention.

13. He will look at your mouth, not just your eyes, when he talks to you. Men have admitted that they look at a woman's mouth and imagine kissing her.

14. If he crosses his leg, it will be in your direction.

15. He will sit or stand within six feet of where you are. This makes him close enough to say something to you.

Fifteen Body Language Signs That Show Your Interest in Him

1. You will smile broadly at him.

2. You will throw him a short, darting glance.

3. You will dance alone to music or snap your fingers in an effort to keep time to the beat of the music.

4. You will look straight at him and flip your hair.

5. You will look at him, toss your head, then look back at him.

6. You will cross and uncross your legs in slow, calculated movements.

7. You will finally cross your upper leg toward him and keep it there.

8. You will begin to thrust or kick your crossed leg up and down.

9. You will dangle your shoe.

10. You will tilt your head slightly and touch your exposed neck.

11. You will casually expose your wrist.

12. You will lick your lips slightly during eye contact.

13. You will primp while keeping eye contact.

14. While walking, you will use exaggerated hip movements.

15. If close enough, you will accidentally brush up against him.

All of the previously mentioned methods are the more traditional approaches to show or understand a partner's interest. But Jan says an unorthodox attempt at acknowledging or discerning his affections can also be used. "You may not even realize it, but objects are often used to invade another person's space and test his or her level of intimacy." According to Jan, pens, wineglasses, cigarettes, or candles can be slid across tabletops, as if they were chess pieces being sent as ambassadors on a mission to represent your heart's desire. Try this: While enjoying a romantic, candlelight dinner, slide a pen, lighter, or glass over the halfway mark of the table into his space. His reaction will be telling.

Jan explains, "If he takes hold of the object and strokes it, or keeps touching it, then he is attracted to you. If he pushes the object back onto your side of the table, you should back off and accept the fact that romance may not be in the cards or on the chessboard for you." Apparently, this is a subconscious action but a clear hint to you that to win at chess, you need to slow down your moves.

Jan warns that not every action that takes place is meant to let you know he's into you or that you are into him. "A good rule of thumb in the realm of nonverbal communication is called the Rule." She continues, "It says: 'To be sure that another person is communicating unequivocal nonverbal sexual interest in you, he or she must be displaying a minimum of four separate positive signals simultaneously, and these signals must be directed at you.'"

Your Body Is Speaking Volumes

Give yourself a hand (and foot and leg, torso, or forearm). You now have the tools to take or make a smile, stance, or glance speak volumes. These nonverbal sexual signals work as a trifecta of sorts. They can guide men from flashing you mixed messages to confirming their interest in you, clue men into your lackluster interest in them, or help you realize that the open party invitation you may think you are sending out may actually say "private party." Your language of love is written all over your body. Use it.

twenty-nine

Texting and Emailing

Dating Under In-text-ication
and E-troductions

They were introduced via cell phones. Chris mostly used shorthand for a quick and easy-to-read text missive, nothing too cutesy or contrived, but convenient and somewhat correct nonetheless. His first text to her was this: "Hey Debbie! It's Chris. I'm lookn' fwd 2 mtng u tonight. This day has been way too long. A good glass of wine will help me 'whine' less 4 sure. What time is good 4 u? Where do u want 2 meet?"

She responded with this: "Your funny. I now...its been way to long for me to. Tonite is great. Let's meet when I'm done work around 6? Do you now were the Wine Exchange is at? Wanna meet their at 6:30?"

Chris wrote back, "Okay, c u there."

Chris was worried about the spelling errors in Debbie's message, but pushed aside his concerns and met her that night anyway. They ordered a bottle of white because "cha-bliss" was her "fave." After a few drinks, Debbie announced, "I'm done my wine. Are you done yours?" Chris flinched. He wanted so badly to correct her. He thought, "We aren't 'done' in an oven. I'm *finished with* my wine, and you are *finished with* yours."

"Wanna go get dinner?" Debbie asked.

Dinner?! Chris couldn't imagine sitting for even another sip, much less an entire meal. He paid the bill and faked a yawn. But in hopes of ending the date ASAP and poking a bit of fun at her, Chris sarcastically said to Debbie, "Gotta go home. It's an oven in here, and I'm done my day."

Debbie didn't get it. Surprise, surprise.

Spell Correctly or Read the Writing on the Wall

When being introduced to a guy, often your text messages, IMs, or emails will be his first real impression of you. They can make or break you, especially if your beauty isn't there to distract and ultimately mask your myriad misspelled missives.

"If I meet a girl out and we exchange numbers, I will shoot her two text messages the next day," says twenty-seven-year-old Juan. "The first is to see if she is interested. The second, wittier one is to see if I am!" Spelling, grammar, and wit are now part of his chase. "A witty repartee is so sexy," he says. "It keeps you wondering, keeps you on your toes, and makes the dating game all the more interesting. I'd rather not waste my time on a girl that doesn't 'get' my humor from the get-go," he says. "If she can't spell or text-banter with me in the beginning, when she has time to think about what she is going to say, then how is a real conversation going to keep me interested?"

Take note. Most men make some conversation concessions when it comes to women, who often use various cutesy ways of shortening words, such as phrases like "c u l8r," "btw," or "lol." Slow down: If you get too cutesy, they could get lost in translation. (How's he supposed to know that "pimp" means you were laughing so hard you meant "peeing in my pants"?) Plus, cutesy can get you caught in linguistic limbo. Some men are so persnickety they even parse words *and* letters. For instance, if you are going to shorten "your," the *u* and *r* should sit together, "ur." If you are trying to shorten the already shortened version of "you are" or "you're," then you should write "u (space) r."

You need to learn his love language and how to wit your way into his heart. Words may lead you to a man that will be the perfect match for your personality. Text messages and writing in general can be a lot like reading tea leaves. Oftentimes if you look at the meaning of his message, you'll be able to predict a lot about your futures, either together or apart.

A Text Test for Love

Take for instance this texting twosome.

Her friends had nicknamed her "the textress." Thirty-two-year-old Casey was amazingly adept at composing some of the best, most pointed, and witty texts, not only to the men she dated but also to her friends and colleagues. Despite her wordy ways, Casey had continued to miss the mark on finding a match. She explained to her friends that she wasn't asking for a brawny brainiac, but at least someone who knew a possessive from a contraction. Her litany of pet-peeve grammar gaffes included using "your" instead of "you're," "its" rather than "it's," and "to" where "too" should be. Date after date she found fault. Many misspellings later, she finally met her linguistic equal, or so she thought.

He was a bachelor-about-town, tall, dark, and "doctored"—a radiologist named Dr. Rossman. After serendipitously bumping into each other a few times, the two agreed via text to meet on purpose at an upcoming party. There was a lively tête-à-tête that included the following set of coquettish texts upon their departure from the party.

CASEY: "I'm leaving. Is there a Dr. in the house?"

DR. ROSSMAN: "No . . . but there can be. Your house?☺"

CASEY: "Ha! Not! But, at least you used the correct 'there' there."

DR. ROSSMAN: "Yes, of course I did—lol! Your to funny!"

Casey was quick to judge, thinking, *No! It couldn't be! Dr. Rossman was another possessed, under-emphatic texter?* Then her friend pointed out, "Maybe he's figured out your humor and was kidding!" The "textress" was transfixed. Could it be that Dr. Rossman used the wrong "your" and "to" to be funny? Turns out he did. The two dated for a good three-month run.

Go Ahead, Read into It

Although men may not be able to verbally express their feelings as well as women, at times their text messages can tell you a lot more than they ever could. You just have to know how to read into things.

"This may be the one aspect of dating in which analysis is actually a good thing," says Dr. Nancy Broz, an English and education professor at Fairleigh Dickinson University. She explains that grammar, spelling, and the ability to relay your personality through the written word has never been more important in the dating world. "Technology has helped us spell-check our way to a country full of bad spellers with poor grammar." However, Dr. Broz explains that technology is also the driving force behind people having to use more spelling and grammar than ever! "This is just the beginning. If you are single and can't spell, you better learn. Technology is multi-plying messaging. To name a few: text messages, Instant Messenger, email, postings on social networking sites, chat rooms, blogs, and Internet dating sites.

In fact, when it comes to Internet dating sites, a good-looking picture may be worth a million hits on your personal profile page, but words can mean even more. In dating chat rooms, droves of men complain of meeting women on dating sites with great-looking pictures who can't seem to worry about grammar, spelling, and punctuation. The men who are worth their salt notice these shortcomings. Thirty-eight-year-old Laurence tells of how he recently read the bio of a former girlfriend on a popular online dating site. "I was amazed at the multitude of misspellings and grammatical mistakes. Instinctively I always realized that there was some sort of gap that existed between us; I just could never identify what it was." He follows up with this: "Upon reading her bio and reflecting, I now realize that these spelling and grammar mistakes were probably evidence of that gap."

Excessive Emails

Another place men get fixated on the faults of women is in their inbox. Apparently, emailing a man can be the end of you before your relationship even begins. "Men have a definitive way of communicating. Think succinctly," says Dr. Broz. Men think linearly. "Too much information will just confuse and annoy them." Women read email and then reread. Men read email and then delete. If you plan on pouring your heart out, you better do it in just five sentences. "A five-sentence email is generally a good length for most men; any more and they start to skim and glaze over, missing the meaning."

Men read email for business. They search for actionable information, not emotion. Bullet points or numbered lists with actionable items such as "do this," "I need this," or "meet here at this time" are all good. If you want to remind him that you are thinking of him, do it directly with one sentence: "I am thinking of you." Period. You also need to be prepared to get no response. His viewpoint is: "There is no 'action' required, and she knows I feel the same way." Hence, a woman's need of expression is a man's idea of redundancy.

"You should also consider the timing of your emails," according to Dr. Broz. The following times will give you the best timing for his undivided (short) attention:

8:00 a.m. to 10:00 a.m.: First thing in the morning almost guarantees the message will be overlooked and forgotten. He is just arriving to work at this time and generally has a full inbox.

11:30 a.m. to 2:30 p.m.: Right after a meeting or before lunch isn't a good time, either. He may have just gotten out of a high-pressured meeting and has to shoot off some emails pertaining to the meeting.

2:30 p.m. to 4:30 p.m.: Late afternoon could be the answer. He most likely has a bit of a lull before the last-minute tasks from his boss pour into his inbox. Keep it short.

7:00 p.m. to 12:00 a.m.: After dinner and later into the night are useless emails. They just add to the gargantuan number of emails collecting in his inbox for the next morning.

5:00 a.m. to 8:00 a.m.: Early mornings can be a good window. Before leaving the house, he may read his email while checking the markets or enjoying his morning paper and coffee. But if you plan on pushing his buttons a bit, this is the worst time for him and ultimately for you. So keep it kind or never mind.

All right, now that you are in the know about what to write, when to write, and how to write any man any message, it's time to put it into practice. Whether it's an email or a text, a blog or a bio, don't let your hands get out of hand. Focus those fumbling fingers on finding your mistakes and fixing them fast. The following list contains some of the most common mistakes men say women make all too often while trying to communicate with them. Before he does the walking because your fingers did the wrong type of talking, take some time to review this table:

Ms.-takes That Drive the "Mr." Crazy

Word	Explanation	Example
Your	Possessive of you	*Your car.*
You're	Contraction of "you are"	*You're happy.*
There	A place	*Sit there.*
Their	Possessive (ownership)	*Their car.*
They're	Contraction of "they are"	*They're not going.*
To	Preposition meaning direction	*To the store.*
Too	Adverb meaning "also" or "too much"	*Too tall.*
Two	Number 2; one plus one	
A lot	Two words—"a" and "lot"—meaning "many"	*I have a lot of DVDs.*

Word	Explanation	Example
Where	In or at what place, in what respect?	*Where did I put my keys?*
Were	Past tense of "are"	*They were here.*
We're	Contraction of "we are"	*We're on our way!*
Than	Conjunction used to compare two people or objects	*I am stronger than he.*
Then	Adverb meaning "at that time"	*Go to the store, then pick up the groceries.*
Lose	Verb form for "loss"	*Did they lose the game?*
Loose	Free, not together	*The animals broke loose.*
Its	Possessive (ownership)	*The school is proud of its team.*
It's	Contraction of "it is"	*It's a long way to the club.*
Whose	Possessive (ownership)	*Whose jacket is on the chair?*
Who's	Contraction of "who is"	*Who's writing the novel?*
Who vs. That	"Who" refers to a person; "that" refers to an object	*He is the man who brought that cake.*
Affect	Verb; to influence or change	*This could affect your future.*
Effect	Noun; the result of	*The effect of the tainted water.*

Word	Explanation	Example
Few	Not many but more than one	*I went to his house for a few minutes.*
Less	Lower in consideration, rank, or importance	*It is less painful than anticipated.*
Over	Above in place or position	*I am so over him.*
More than	A quantifier meaning greater in size or amount or extent or degree	*There are more than fifty men on your dance card.* Not: *There are over fifty . . .*
Alright	Not a word!	
All right	Correct spelling	*It is all right with me.*
Altogether	Means "entirely"	*She doesn't altogether approve of me.*
All together	Means "in the same place"	*We were all together at the holidays.*
Right	Correct in judgment, opinion, or action	*You made the right decision.*
Correct	To set or make true, accurate, or right; to remove the errors or faults from	*He corrected my grammatical error.*
Finished	To complete something	*The task is finished.*
Done	Cooked sufficiently	*The cake is done.*
Quiet	Adjective: still, silent	*The room was quiet.*

Word	Explanation	Example
Quit	Verb; to stop doing something	*I quit my job.*
Quite	Adverb: completely, very	*She was quite entertaining.*
Receive, Believe	You know the meaning, but can you spell them?	*Remember the "i before e, except after c" rule?*
Would of	Incorrect! No such wording! "Of" can't be used in this way	*What you mean is "would've," a contraction for "would have."*
Should of	Incorrect	*Should have.*
Could of	Incorrect	*Could have.*
Dam	Noun; a barrier to obstruct the flow of water	*The beaver built a dam.*
Damn	Verb; to swear, to curse	*Damn. He looks good!*
Tonight	Noun; this present or coming night	*Can you go tonight?*
Tonite	Noun; an explosive compound, the preparation of gun cotton	*Bam! You blew that up with tonite!*
May	Auxiliary verb; used to express possibility	*May I go shopping?*
Can	Verb; to be able to, to have the ability or power to	*Can you feel the love tonight?*

Word	Explanation	Example
Right	Adjective; correct in judgment, opinion, or action	*You are so right!*
Write	Verb; to inscribe	*Write it out for me.*
Rite	Noun; a formal or ceremonial act or procedure	*She performed a sacrificial rite.*
Sight	Noun; an instance of seeing	*What a beautiful sight.*
Site	The position or location of an object in relation to its environment	*He is at the construction site.*
Cite	Verb; to refer to as support or confirmation for an argument	*She cited* The Man Plan *to support her claim that guys like vanilla perfume.*
Real	Existing or occurring as a fact; true; the opposite of fake	*Her boobs are real.*
Really	Adverb; actually, genuinely, truly	*Her boobs are really fake.*
Threw	Past tense of the verb "throw"; to fling, launch, or send	*He threw the football into the stands.*
Thru	Informal spelling of "through"	*We went thru New York on our way to Boston.*

Word	Explanation	Example
Through	Adjective; about, across, ended, finished. Adverb; over, around	*Our relationship was through by the time we were through Boston.*
Thorough	Adjective; full, complete, meticulous, detailed, exact	*Her analysis of the situation was thorough.*
At	Never end a sentence with the preposition "at"	*Where are you?* Not: *Where are you at?*
Took	"Took" is never spelled with an "e"— "toke"—unless you are doing just that…	*He took a toke.*

A Lasting Linguistic Lesson: Abbreviations

One final note worth noting while sending notes via text or email: Abbreviations are acceptable forms of communication, especially if you have a traditional phone without a full keypad. However, this tech caveat should be relayed early in the textual relationship. Some acceptable abbreviations worth noting are omg (oh my god), btw (by the way), w. e. (whatever), r (are), u (you), ur (your), u r (you're), ROTFL (rolling on the floor laughing), LOL (laugh out loud), LMAO (laughing my a★★ off), WTF (what the #$%!), 2nite (tonight), L8r (later), Rt (right), Plz (please), and Sry (sorry). Be warned: Don't get 2 carried away with the abrev., 2 much 2 soon can lead 2 him saying 2 u, "L8r G8r!" PIMP (peeing in my pants!).

thirty

High Maintenance

Coffee Before Commitment

While studying for the bar, twenty-nine-year-old Jack spent a lot of time at the coffee shop a few blocks from his house where he could also study all the hot girls who frequented the place. He was particularly keen on one woman. "Her name was Gretchen," Jack says. "She had to be a model or something; she was really that beautiful." One day he decided he was going to introduce himself. "I walked up to her in the line and offered to buy her a 'cup-o-joe.'" Jack then waited while she ordered. "I think it may have taken twenty minutes for her to tell the dude her order." To the best of his recollection, it went something like this:

COFFEE DUDE: "May I take your order?"

GRETCHEN: "Yes, I'd like a large glass of ice, half filled with regular coffee, not iced coffee, but coffee over ice. The other half—halved with equal parts skim milk and half-and-half, then add one pump of sugar-free caramel flavoring and one pump of sugar-free vanilla flavoring, finishing it off with one package of Equal and one package of Splenda."

Jack remembers the dialogue so vividly because it was the only day in his life that he ever thought a hot model actually looked not-so-hot. "She lost her luster with that ridiculous order."

Difficult versus Definite, High Maintenance versus Knowing What You Want

It is clear that men have issues with high-maintenance women. What's happening in a man's head when he hears a woman order like this? Well, according to men, in addition to thinking that one day the woman may demand that they order that exact crazy coffee concoction for her, they also envision her demanding them to pick up everything for her—from her tampons to her tofu. Less is more for men; not a lesser woman but a less demanding one.

The 1930s silver-screen stunner Hedy Lamarr once said, "I'm not difficult. I am definite." The actress's concept of being "difficult" may have been to the 1930s what "high mainte-nance" is considered today. "In relationships you are constantly exchanging resources," explains Dr. Suzanne Buck, who teaches graduate classes on subjects such as persuasion, public speaking, and interpersonal communication at the Univer-sity of Houston. "Men perceive these exchanges of resources as costs versus rewards," Dr. Buck says. To a man, when costs (the resources men are giving) greatly exceed their rewards (the resources men receive in the exchange), that's high main-tenance. "It is a nuanced definition, because no two indi-viduals view rewards and costs exactly the same—especially men and women!" Over time, and as relationships develop or change, one individual may have more costs, less rewards, or vice versa, changing the definition of high or low maintenance. When a man's cost is high—that is, he has to use excessive physical, mental, fiscal, and/or emotional effort to sustain the relationship just to receive the reward—that's when a man may hit the road.

To men, this reward-to-cost ratio boils down to winners versus losers. High-maintenance women are perceived to want to "one-up" all the time. The further the relationship progresses, the more investment is required from him to help her one-up her growing list of one-ups.

It seems contradictory when men say they want a woman who takes care of herself physically, dresses nicely, and is refined. They think, "If she takes good care of herself, then she will probably take good care of me." But in the same breath, they complain about women who primp and preen and require special care. This special care is often the care that makes women look so good, well dressed, healthy, and refined. How is a woman to know what "acceptable" high-maintenance behavior is and what it isn't?

A man will find a woman more worth the chase if she is attractive, appealing, and admirable, but step over that line and it's game over. To a man, high maintenance is all about keeping a balance. Consider some of the following nuances in some female characteristics that men say are low maintenance and desirable versus characteristics men specifically call high maintenance and undesirable.

His Lookout List: High-Maintenance versus Low-Maintenance Traits

Brainy (shows off/up) versus Intelligent (problem-solves)

Busybody (in your kitchen) versus Social Butterfly, Gregarious (involved)

Bitchy (get it for me) versus Assertive (yes, I can)

Boisterous (noisy) versus Exuberant (lively)

Expensive (draining) versus Luxurious (deserving)

Demanding (whiny, pushy) versus Ambitious (inspired, achiever)

Persnickety (fussy) versus Selective (challenging, stimulating)

Conceited (self-important) versus Cultured (she's got style)

Vain (probably thinks *every* song is about her!) versus Dignified (poised)

Arrogant (haughty, superior) versus Confident (secure)

So now that you know the distinctions between what men perceive as high maintenance and low maintenance, if you find that you are more of the former than the latter, you'll need to correct some common high-maintenance mistakes before any man is really going to enjoy being with you and staying with you. There are a few verbal and nonverbal tips you can apply to your dating life that will help any high-maintenance woman mitigate those potentially negative traits and make the man in her life breathe a sigh of relief.

Watch your facial expressions. Eye contact and touch play an important role in male-female relationships. Women who make direct eye contact and smile are viewed by men as positive, secure, and confident. In addition, women who touch others (in an appropriate manner) more than they touch themselves (in an appropriate manner, wink-wink) are also viewed by men in a positive manner. High-maintenance women normally make less direct eye contact, touch themselves more (adjusting hair, clothing, etc.), and gleam "fake" smiles. Men get the picture and want out of the picture with women like this.

Assess your dress and attire. These outward things provide a lot of clues that lead men to assume a woman is high or low maintenance. Women who are stylish and trendy are viewed as more favorable and desirable by men. Meantime, women who are only interested in being trendy, regardless of style, are usually deemed high maintenance by men. Dressing appropriately for a woman's age is also important. High-maintenance women have a tendency to dress much younger than their actual age. Context sometimes alters these aspects, but generally this is the rule of thumb.

Listen up! Vocal cues are important. Women who want to appear low maintenance to men must project their voice to include soft tones, appropriate inflection, and moderate speech rates. Variations of these elements combined with proper articulation, enunciation, and pronunciation further enhance a women's ability to appear low maintenance. All elements of rate, pitch, tone, inflection, and even vocal pauses are considered either consciously or subconsciously by men when they are seeking a woman to date or mate.

Your gestures give you away. As discussed in the previous chapter, elements of nonverbal communication such as body language are also used by men to measure credibility, trustworthiness, power, and sincerity—all part of weeding out the high-maintenance women from the low-maintenance ones. Men view women who make moderate gestures (waving/signaling friends, nodding their head, etc.) as confident and secure. This is especially important with a woman's walk. If she walks with her head high, her arms out, and long strides, men will take more notice. Women who exaggerate gestures and movement (swinging hair, dramatic facial expressions, hand gestures that look more like wings flapping) are viewed by men as less credible, less powerful, and insincere—aka high maintenance. If a woman maintains correct posture (standing up straight with arms open), she is showing a man she can stand on her own in a good way. If she has a slouched-over or closed posture (hands on hips, or closed arms across the breast with one leg bent), this leads men to perceive her as less confident and therefore more needy, which is considered high maintenance.

Talk less, listen more. Men view women who talk more about themselves in a bragging manner to be high maintenance without a doubt. At the other end of the spectrum, women who talk about themselves in an extremely negative manner (poor, pitiful me) may also be viewed as high maintenance— given that they appear weak, insecure, and needy. In addition, women who talk extensively about money are usually viewed as high maintenance.

If You Can't Beat 'Em, Join 'Em!

It is clear that men expect women to require a relative amount of maintaining. Like attracts like; if you find you just can't budge in the maintenance department, then find a guy who uses more than three types of hair products and knows the name and brand of each one. This metrosexual-type guy may be so into himself he won't notice how into yourself you are.

thirty-one

Commitment Issues

Are We Dating . . . or What?

It had been two months, and twenty-five-year-old Rebecca wanted to know, "Are we dating, or what?" The pressure was mounting. She wanted, needed, no, she *deserved* to know. Her answer came shortly after Charlie, her man-in-question, popped the question, asking, "Will you . . . go to this wedding with me?" She said, "Yes," only to find her real answer was a big "N-O!"

Charlie explains: "I was introducing her to one of my friends and totally blanked when I said, 'I'd like to introduce you to my . . . my . . . umm [pause] . . . I'd like to introduce you to Rebecca.'" Ouch. Charlie could see it in Rebecca's face. It was too late. His introduction might just as well have been his good-bye. "She barely talked to me for the rest of the reception," Charlie says. "Plus, she ended up storming off into the night because I went to the bar and forgot to bring her a drink, too. It was only a drink!" But as incredulous as he plays it, Charlie knew why Rebecca took off. She wanted to know what the deal was with their deal. Were they for real? To which Charlie flippantly replies, "Nowadays, if you don't ask a woman for her hand in marriage after the second date, she'll storm off into the night."

Rebecca had her own take on the matter: "From what I can gather...he wants to be my only one, but he wants to have more than one." She was right. Charlie had been dating more women than just Rebecca. She was devastated. While consoling her, a friend asked if, during the two-month courtship, she had ever asked Charlie the "Are we exclusive?" question. "No way!" she barked. Truth be told, she had asked, but the thought of admitting it made Rebecca's face turn as red as a sheet. Especially because she had discovered other women were also between his sheets! She called Charlie for an explanation. His response was short and scathing. "I don't like to be pressured into anything. When I'm ready to date you exclusively, I'll tell you. Until then, it's chill out or get out." Out she went.

It Has to Be Their Idea

Most would listen to the story of Charlie and Rebecca and say, "Duh!" Every woman knows that the competitive-hunting nature of men doesn't respond well to pressure from the commitment-gathering nature of females. No matter, some women will continue to pressure, while most men will continue to flee.

This last lesson on the concept of commitment (or lack thereof) is a crucial part of the plan. If you are to lure, captivate, and win over men in order to drive them wild, then you have to stop trying to divine the differences between hangin' out, hookin' up, and dating men. This is a dangerous dance— the kind in which if you step on his toes, he's liable to leave you *and* his shoes on the dance floor to go tear it up barefoot with some other girl. The lesson here is: Resist the temptation to push for a relationship explanation. But if you falter, when you step on his toes, make sure you're wearing very pointy and sexy four-inch stilettos!

Slow Dancing

Jenifer Beckman, a well-known marriage and family therapist from the Center for Counseling, offers some very pointed advice. "Slow down. You have to know your dance partner's moves well before you try to tango with the commitment question." Jenifer adds, "There's a reason why the man usually leads. Let go and let him." According to Jenifer, if your man has some fancy footwork and always dances around opportunities to make a commitment, chances are he's just not ready to commit, or it's time to face the music...you may not be the one. "If he continues to not commit, putting pressure on him will only make him more determined to hold on to his freedom. It is a subconscious response." She also warns that "if you stick around waiting, that's your prerogative. But by staying, you are condoning his commitment phobia. He won't respect that. Your risk of getting hurt will then increase exponentially." In other words, dance at your own risk.

"It's not foolproof, but it's not foolhardy, either," Jenifer says, explaining that there are five factors you should consider before you'll know whether you are in a healthy, committed relationship. The first of her five is "the quality and quantity count." She explains: "You need to see a lot of the person and share a lot with the person—not just facts but feelings." Second, it's all about your location, location, location. Jenifer says long-distance dating is not only geographically undesirable but proverbially "bad on the heart." The third factor includes "having plans without making plans." The fourth factor—you've met the family, friends, and Fido. "You should get along with at least two out of the three!" Jenifer says. Finally, she admonishes, "Communicate—it should never just be 'understood.' Be patient, open, and observant." Then when the timing is right, let *him* ask the question: "Are we dating...or what?" Your answer will be, "Of course we are."

Committing to Mastery of the Man Plan

Congratulations! You've completed the final step in the man plan. That's real commitment! Now you have all the tools to lure him in, captivate, and then conquer his senses and attention. Go ahead, drive him wild if you want. The steps in the man plan have let you in on the mind of men. They are easy codes to crack when you have formed the right attack. If you've put to practice all of the adjusting, tinkering, and fine-tuning the man plan has suggested, you are well on your way to revolutionizing and revitalizing both your physical and your practical approach to all men. You are empowered; you are victorious.

After you celebrate victory, remember vigilance. You need to be vigilant with every step along the way. Stay the course of the man plan. You have learned that you should sweat the small stuff so as to enjoy the bigger picture when it comes to men. If you do, then look out, ladies! Not only will you drive him wild, but you will also learn how to keep him there. You may have chosen his adventure in the beginning of the man plan, but now you're ending up on your own. Now *that's* a plan.

acknowledgments

A good friend will love your idea for a new book—a great friend will love *you* enough to make you believe you can actually write one. I have great friends; starting with a group of dedicated, kind, and unwavering women (and one man) who introduced me to a kind of happiness and loyalty that few will ever know. They are KHOU-TV's finest, my producers and friends at *Great Day Houston*: Kim Gagne, Sabrina Miskelly, Cristina Terrill, Meredith Baker, Rebecca Spera, Chris Nocera, Tiffany Rubio, Michelle Rexroat, and Amaris Salinas. I want to also thank the higher-ups at Belo, including Peter Diaz, Susan McEldoon, and Don Graham, for making it possible for me to meet and work with this amazingly talented TV family. Without their input, I could never have created this book.

My "other family" is the group of friends who read chapters, called-in favors, listened to my crazy concerns, cared, supported, and unwaveringly loved me through this book-writing process. I know that no matter what I am, do, or decide to be when I grow up they will always be there for me. These are the friends who care about me even when I don't call back (but text?): Cindi and Mike Avila, Amanda Wells, Diane Stidham, Diane Gordan, Tracy Stanton, Shad Azimi, Carlton Hudson (and her mom and dad, Peggie and Jerry Cohen), and last, my dad and his amazing wife—Charlie and Lynda Casey.

In addition, those friends with big jobs and big titles (who just want to use their "bigness" to help make you "bigger") are some of the most generous and helpful people to call friends. Those friends are people like John Demsey, Bonnie Fuller, Suze Yalof Schwartz, and Leslie Stevens. John helped develop "the Whitney Plan" to go along with *The Man Plan*. Thank you, John, for the title, cover, and conviction. You gave me the first two; the third one is an evolving part of "the Whitney Plan." Bonnie has always made herself available for quick questions, coffee klatches, and kick-arse quotes. You are an inspiring and steadfast role model. Suze gives great quote, too, but as an author herself, she also let me know this: "You have to do if for the love of the game...whatever comes after is just extra!" So, thanks Suze, for the "extra" help with your magazine. Finally, Leslie gave me guidance, advice, an "expert" title, and a group of girls to chat me up as said expert (Emily and Jennifer from LaForce & Stevens, you rule!).

When it comes to friends and their roles, having an editor as a friend can present a precarious position of sorts. With one hand, er, keystroke, they are fastidiously chopping, deleting, rearranging, and reworking what you think is your pièce de rèsistance. But it is what my editor, Meg Leder, did with her other hand that makes her a true genius in the editing world. Meg would know just when to pat me on the back with her best "go get 'em, girl" encouraging email or call. Her brilliance is her ability to own the content and decision making by sharing it back with the author; every decision, deletion, and dilemma is a team effort. Meg detests dogma. She is smart, beautiful, witty, and she let me keep "Hey, Hey, Her Vajayjay" in the book, which clearly makes her "way kewl." Meg also introduced me to Jeanette Shaw, who was a peppy and intuitive third brain for both of us. Can you imagine, a blonde with three brains? Hello, genius! I am so grateful to you Meg—forever.

Speaking of editors, I couldn't have realized my dream of writing 60,000 words without that 800-word newspaper deadline every week. Thank you to Kyrie O'Conner and Melissa Aguilar from the *Houston Chronicle*; you both give me the freedom and the foundation to write my heart out, weekly. Because of you, I'll never forget what opportunity looks like and how many emails it takes to get one.

It was both emails and opportunity that created the next chapter...literally. The *Houston Chronicle* gave me a weekly column. Someone special read that column weekly via email. One day he wrote a simple email back to me that said, "Have you ever thought of writing a book?" Four months after that email, my literary agent Glen Hartley and I were in his New York office when the first image of *The Man Plan*'s cover came into his email inbox. Voilà! A book had been born. Thank you, Glen, for sifting through the six-foot-tall, blond subterfuge and saying, "Whitney, you have a native brilliance." Er, I think that brilliance is *you*, Glen!

Encouragement and loyalty like Glen's come from a special type of person. Two other people in my lifetime have believed in me on a professional level like that. They are a part of my life like a dynamic-duo superhero team—there when you need them in a flash, but hoping all along they have already given you all the tools and powers you will ever need to fight crime solo. I met them both when I was a young-cub reporter at WTVJ-TV in Miami. Thank you, Don Browne and Ike Seamans. We did it!

Finally to my mom, Barbara Casey—you made all of the aforementioned people, places, and things possible. Every single part of my life has been touched, influenced, and made better by you. I love you. Always.

index

You've read Match.com
Relationship Insider
Whitney Casey's *The Man Plan*.
Now put it into action with
2 Weeks Free on Match.com!

Redeem your free trial on
Match.com, the world's largest
online dating community.

**Go to
www.match.com/manplan
and get your 2 WEEKS FREE today!**

match.com®